At the Heart of the Gospel

Christopher West is to be commended for the courage and strength of conviction with which he proclaims, upholds, and defends the spousal vision of the Church, particularly as it's articulated in John Paul II's Theology of the Body. It's with great enthusiasm as his diocesan bishop that I endorse this magnificent book and recommend it to a wide, wide readership.

—Most Reverend Joseph P. McFadden
Bishop of Harrisburg
Chairman, USCCB Committee on Catholic Education

Inspiring, compelling, faithful and compassionate—*At the Heart of the Gospel* invites us to follow in the footsteps of Blessed John Paul II as authentic witnesses of the truth and beauty of the Gospel amid the many challenges of contemporary culture. A must-read for everyone involved in the new evangelization!

—Most Reverend Kevin C. Rhoades
Bishop of Fort Wayne–South Bend
Chairman, USCCB Committee on Laity, Marriage, Family Life and Youth

Christopher West has gone to the desert . . . and come back stronger than ever. Those who may previously have thought his work was one-sided in its celebration of the body and sexuality will find here, brought out more clearly than ever, the deep balance and integration that has always been the foundation of his work.

—Most Reverend Robert J. Carlson
Archbishop of Saint Louis
Chairman, USCCB Committee on Clergy, Consecrated Life and Vocations

As a former professor of West's, I may be biased in his favor, but I can honestly say that he has taught me a great deal through this magnificently developed and theologically sound work. His balanced and insightful analyses make it clear that West has immersed himself in the great mystics, Fathers, and doctors of the Church. His treatment of a delicate question of foreplay by married couples is perhaps the finest I have ever read. In short, this is a magnificent theological work that ought to be widely read by all interested in the Theology of the Body and the new evangelization.

—William E. May

Emeritus Michael J. McGivney Professor of Moral Theology at the Pontifical John Paul II Institute for Studies on Marriage and Family at the Catholic University of America

West's highly anticipated work *At the Heart of the Gospel* is in keeping with the man I have come to know and respect since our close collaboration on the new English translation of TOB. In short, this balanced and judicious work demonstrates what I have long understood: West knows John Paul II's TOB as few others do and he shows great theological skill in presenting, explaining, and upholding the late pope's teaching. He grasps its letter with remarkable completeness and is led faithfully by its spirit. He is to be commended for his courage in defending John Paul II's teaching (and the theological tradition upon which it's based) in the face of strong opposition.

—Michael Waldstein

Max Seckler Professor of Theology, Ave Maria University

The beatification of Pope John Paul II is more than the Church's official recognition of his sanctity. John Paul II's teaching is now bequeathed to the Church in a new way—not only by his authority as Pope, but also by his personal experience of sanctity. Christopher West is an authentic witness to the transformative power of John Paul II's teaching and this book accurately captures the meaning of his Theology of the Body and its critical importance for the new evangelization.

—Monsignor Lorenzo Albacete

Theologian, Author, and Founding Professor of the John Paul II Institute for Studies on Marriage and Family, Washington, D.C.

Why should you read this book? Because Christopher West is the "translator" of Pope John Paul the Great's Theology of the Body into clear, simple, popular language; and the Theology of the Body is the Church's answer to the great heresy of our time, the "Sexual Revolution"; and the Sexual Revolution is the main cause of the corruption and decline of marriage and the family; and the family is the primary key to the health of any civilization; and our civilization is already halfway to "Brave New World." *At the Heart of the Gospel* provides the alternative.

—Peter Kreeft

Professor of Philosophy, Boston College

Theology of the Body is John Paul II's synthesis and analysis of the Church's theological tradition on what it means to be human. *At the Heart of the Gospel* is a book that provides an intellectually clear summary, synthesis, analysis, and catechism of John Paul II's Theology of the Body. As a professor of homiletics I consider this book a guiding light for how to proclaim the gospel to the modern world. It is Christopher West's *Apologia Pro Vita Sua.*

—Fr. Fred Gaglia

Professor of Homiletics, St. John Vianney Theological Seminary, Denver

If complacency in the Church is a sleeping lion, then one can expect many swipes of the paw at the work of Christopher West. *At the Heart of the Gospel* compellingly demonstrates the truth of the matter: West is bringing fresh grace to both the Church and the wider culture. With the wisdom born of trial and the humble acceptance of his own poverty, West targets our aching need and directs us to healing with surgical precision. His proclamation of the Gospel is joyous, contemporary, and contagious! Onward Christopher, we are listening!

—Anne, a lay apostle

Direction for Our Times; Author, Lessons in Love

ALSO BY CHRISTOPHER WEST

Good News about Sex and Marriage: Answers to Your Honest Questions about Catholic Teaching (Servant, 2000; revised edition 2006)

Theology of the Body Explained: A Commentary on John Paul II's Man and Woman He Created Them (Pauline, 2003; revised edition, 2007)

Theology of the Body for Beginners: A Basic Introduction to John Paul II's Sexual Revolution (Ascension Press, 2004; revised edition, 2009)

The Love that Satisfies: Reflections on Eros and Agape (Ascension Press, 2007)

Heaven's Song: Sexual Love as It Was Meant to Be (Ascension Press, 2008)

At the Heart of the Gospel

Reclaiming the Body for the New Evangelization

Christopher West

Image Books
New York

Published in the United States by Image Books, an imprint of the Crown Publishing Group, a division of Random House, Inc., New York.

IMAGE and the Image colophon are registered trademarks of Random House, Inc.

Library of Congress cataloging-in-publication data is available upon request.

Nihil Obstat:	William E. May, Ph.D.
Imprimatur:	Joseph Patrick McFadden
	Bishop of Harrisburg
	September 22, 2011

ISBN 978-0-307-98711-2
eISBN 978-0-307-98712-9

PRINTED IN THE UNITED STATES OF AMERICA

Cover design by Jen O'Connor
Cover photography by David Kang

10 9 8 7 6 5 4 3 2 1

First Edition

To David Savage, Matthew Pinto, and Maria Stumpf,
with deep gratitude for all you have done for me.

CONTENTS

Abbreviations

ACM — *An Anthology of Christian Mysticism,* edited by Harvey D. Egan, 2nd edition (Liturgical Press, 1996)

BES — *Beatitudes: Eight Steps to Happiness,* Father Raniero Cantalamessa (Servant, 2009)

BNA — *Be Not Afraid,* interview with Pope John Paul II by Andre Frossard (Image Books, 1985)

BSCT — *The Beatitudes: Soundings in Christian Tradition,* Simon Tugwell O.P. (Templegate, 1980)

CCC — *Catechism of the Catholic Church* (Libreria Editrice Vaticana, 1997)

CE — *The Catholic Encyclopedia,* Volume XIV (The Encyclopedia Press, 1913)

CL — *Covenant of Love,* Richard Hogan and John LeVoir (Ignatius Press, 1992)

CMHS — *The Christian Meaning of Human Sexuality,* Paul Quay S.J. (Ignatius Press, 1985)

CSE — *Catholic Sexual Ethics,* Ronald Lawler, Joseph Boyle, William May, 2nd edition (Our Sunday Visitor, 1998)

CTH — *Crossing the Threshold of Hope,* Pope John Paul II (Knopf, 1994)

DC — *Deus Caritas Est,* Pope Benedict XVI's Encyclical Letter God Is Love (Pauline, 2006)

DM — *Dives in Misericordia,* Pope John Paul II's Encyclical Letter on Divine Mercy (Pauline, 1980)

EKH — *Everything You Ever Wanted to Know about Heaven,* Peter Kreeft (Ignatius Press, 1990)

ES — *Ecclesiam Suam,* Pope Paul VI's Encyclical Letter on the Church (Pauline, 1964)

EV — *Evangelium Vitae,* Pope John Paul II's Encyclical Letter The Gospel of Life (Pauline, 1995)

FC	*Familiaris Consortio,* Pope John Paul II's Apostolic Exhortation on the Role of the Christian Family in the Modern World (Pauline, 1981)
FR	*Fides et Ratio,* Pope John Paul II's Encyclical Letter on Faith and Reason (Pauline, 1998)
FS	*Through the Year with Bishop Fulton Sheen,* Henry Dieterich (Ignatius Press, 2003)
GNSM	*Good News About Sex and Marriage,* Christopher West, revised edition (Servant, 2006)
GR	*God at the Ritz: Attraction to Infinity,* Lorenzo Albacete (Crossroads, 2002)
GS	*Gaudium et Spes,* Vatican II's Pastoral Constitution on the Church in the Modern World (Pauline, 1965)
GW	*The Grain of Wheat: Aphorisms,* Hans Urs von Balthasar (Ignatius Press, 1995)
HS	*Heaven's Song: Sexual Love as It Was Meant to Be,* Christopher West (Ascension Press, 2008)
IF	*Interior Freedom,* Jacques Philippe (Scepter Publishers, 2007)
JN2	*Jesus of Nazareth Part II,* Pope Benedict XVI (Ignatius Press, 2011)
LA	*Letter to Artists,* Pope John Paul II (Pauline, 1999)
LF	*Letter to Families,* Pope John Paul II (Pauline, 1994)
LR	*Love and Responsibility,* Karol Wojtyla (Ignatius Press, 1981)
LS	*The Love That Satisfies: Reflections on Eros and Agape,* Christopher West (Ascension Press, 2007)
LW	*Light of the World,* Pope Benedict XVI (Ignatius Press, 2010)
MCS	*Mary: The Church at the Source,* Hans Urs von Balthasar and Joseph Ratzinger (Ignatius Press, 2005)
MD	*Mulieris Dignitatem,* Pope John Paul II's Apostolic Letter on the Dignity and Vocation of Women (Pauline, 1988)
MI	*Memory and Identity,* Pope John Paul II (Rizzoli Books, 2005)
NE	*The Nicomachean Ethics,* Aristotle (Oxford University Press, 1992)

NM	*The Nuptial Mystery,* Angelo Scola (Eerdmans, 2005)
NMI	*Novo Millennio Ineunte,* Pope John Paul II's Apostolic Letter at the Close of the Great Jubilee (Pauline, 2001)
OL	*Orientale Lumen,* Pope John Paul II's Encyclical Letter on the Light of the East (Pauline, 1995)
PC	*Person and Community: Selected Essays* (of Karol Wojtyla's), trans. Theresa Sandok (Peter Lang, 1993)
QD	*Questiones de Castitate et Luxuria,* Benoit Merkelbach, 4th edition (La Pensee Catholique, 1936)
RG	*The Reed of God,* Caryll Houselander (Ave Maria Press, 2006)
RH	*Redemptor Hominis,* Pope John Paul II's Encyclical Letter on The Redeemer of Man (Pauline, 1979)
RM	*Redemptoris Missio,* Pope John Paul II's Encyclical Letter on the Mission of the Redeemer (Pauline, 1990)
RW	*Redeemer in the Womb,* John Saward (Ignatius Press, 1993)
SAS	*Sex and Sacredness,* Christopher Derrick (Ignatius Press, 1982)
SD	*Salvifici Dolores,* Pope John Paul II's Encyclical Letter on the Christian Meaning of Suffering (Pauline, 1984)
SL	*The Spirit of the Liturgy,* Joseph Ratzinger (Ignatius Press, 2000)
SMC	*Sex and the Marriage Covenant,* John F. Kippley (Couple to Couple League, 1992)
SMP	*Searching for and Maintaining Peace,* Jacques Philippe (St. Paul's, 2002)
SOS	*Story of a Soul,* Saint Thérèse of Lisieux (ICS Publications, 1976)
SP	*Sermons Preached on Various Occasions,* John Henry Newman (newmanreader.org)
SS	*Spes Salvi,* Pope Benedict XVI's Encyclical Letter Saved in Hope (Pauline, 2007)
TF	"The Two Faces of Love," Father Raniero Cantalamessa, First Lenten Sermon to the Roman Curia, 2011

TM *Theologia Moralis,* Saint Alphonsus Liguori (ed. M. Heilig, 1857)

TOBB *Theology of the Body for Beginners,* Christopher West, revised edition (Ascension Press, 2009)

TOBE *Theology of the Body Explained,* Christopher West, revised edition (Pauline, 2007)

TOB *Man and Woman He Created Them: A Theology of the Body,* Pope John Paul II's general audience addresses on Human Love in the Divine Plan (Pauline, 2006)

TSS *The Song of Songs: As Interpreted by Early Christian and Medieval Commentators,* Richard Norris (Eerdman's, 2003)

VMTB *The Virgin Mary and Theology of the Body,* edited by Donald Calloway, MIC (Marian Press, 2005)

VP *Via Pulchritudinis: Privileged Pathway for Evangelization & Dialogue,* Pontifical Council for Culture (2006)

VS *Veritatis Splendor,* Pope John Paul II's Encyclical Letter on the Splendor of Truth (Pauline, 2003)

WH *Witness to Hope,* George Weigel's biography of Pope John Paul II (Harper Collins, 1999)

FOREWORD

By making us male and female in the divine image, God established a set purpose for our sexuality, ordering us to the intimate sharing of our very being with another person that's open to participating in the creative power of God in bringing about new life. To proclaim this truth today requires courage and strength. And few have dared to engage the culture with Catholic teaching on human sexuality as Christopher West does. For this we can be grateful.

When I was named a bishop, I took as my Episcopal motto, "*Mary the Model, Jesus the Center.*" Mary is the model of openness to Jesus. She is the one who shows us how to bear Christ to others. True to his name, Christopher West is an authentic "Christ-bearer," effective as a teacher and an evangelist. Through an understanding of Pope John Paul II's teaching on the human person, made popular and taught throughout the globe by Christopher West, persons have come back to the practice of their faith, marriages have been strengthened and saved, and vocations to the priesthood and religious life have been fostered and renewed.

Through nearly twenty years of service to the Church, Christopher West has gained a hard-earned wisdom born of a constant "confrontation of doctrine with life," as John Paul II put it (LR, p. 15). In his latest work, *At the Heart of the Gospel,* West shares that hard-earned wisdom with the rest of us, mapping a path toward an effective and "new" evangelization.

In our efforts to share Christ with the world, much is at stake in the way we understand (or fail to understand) the meaning of our bodies. Ours is a faith of "incarnation," in which spiritual truths are revealed *in the flesh.* Indeed, it is the human body "in all its materiality," as Blessed John Paul II wrote, that reveals "who man is (and who he ought to be)" (TOB 7:2). It is in the body, in all its beauty as male and female, that we see a sign of the ultimate vocation of every human being to become "one body, one spirit with Christ." In Jesus, the Word made flesh, God has revealed that man and woman's future is not limited to this world but that we have an eternal destiny in the Marriage of the Lamb (Rev 19:7).

In this way, as Christopher West illuminates so beautifully for us, John Paul II's *Theology of the Body* takes us to the heart of the Gospel itself. The "great mystery" of spousal love frames the entire biblical story. As the *Catechism of the Catholic Church* observes, "Sacred Scripture begins with the creation of man and woman in the image and likeness of God and concludes with a vision of 'the wedding-feast of the Lamb' " (CCC 1602). Christ is the ultimate Bridegroom and the Church is his Bride. In turn, the "entire Christian life bears the mark of the spousal love of Christ and the Church. Already Baptism, the entry into the People of God, is a nuptial mystery; it is so to speak the nuptial bath which precedes the wedding feast, the Eucharist" (CCC 1617).

This means we must allow John Paul II's *Theology of the Body* to inform our understanding not only of the sacrament of marriage, but of all of the sacraments, and of every state of life. We must allow this beautiful theology of spousal love to inform our understanding of the liturgy, the tenets of the Creed, our personal prayer life, our works of charity, and our hope in heaven.

Scholars will explore, expound, and penetrate the finer points of John Paul II's theology for centuries. However, if we are to become authentic witnesses to Blessed John Paul II's teaching, we must take it up not only as a project of academic study, but also (and even more so) as a "project of the heart." At its deepest level, the *Theology of the Body* offers a mystical kind of wisdom. And this means that a merely academic approach can only take a person so far.

As Saint Bonaventure wrote, if one wishes to receive "mystical wisdom," he should "ask grace, not instruction; desire, not understanding; the groaning of prayer, not diligent reading; the Spouse, not the teacher; God, not man; darkness, not clarity; not light, but the fire that totally inflames and carries us into God by ecstatic unctions and burning affections" (*The Soul's Journey into God*).

In Jesus Christ, God comes to us in a way that we can relate to and understand: through a human body, through human love, and through human language. Similarly, if the treasures of John Paul II's *Theology of the Body* are to become accessible to those who need them most, they must be put in a language that average men and women can relate to and understand.

Christopher West has been a pioneer in this task. As he himself admits, finding the right approach and successfully navigating it has been a challenging process. West's determination to persevere is our gain. West's teaching helps the Church to "reclaim the body for the new evangelization." With great clarity and great charity, *At the Heart of the Gospel* shows us how.

At the Heart of the Gospel is the work of a theological mind, but also the fruit of a contemplative heart. Far from a superficial glance, we benefit, as Christopher West has, from prayerfully "receiving" John Paul II's teaching and pondering it deeply. As West makes clear, if we are to live the full truth of our sexuality according to our particular state in life, we must persevere on the interior journey: we must learn to embrace God's purifying fire, find divine strength in our weaknesses, and boast of nothing but the cross of Christ.

Christopher West is an authentic witness to this journey. He is to be commended for the courage and strength of conviction with which he proclaims, upholds, and defends the spousal vision of the Church, particularly as it's articulated in John Paul II's *Theology of the Body.* It's with great enthusiasm as his diocesan bishop that I endorse this magnificent book and recommend it to a wide, wide readership.

Most Reverend Joseph P. McFadden
Bishop of Harrisburg
Chairman, USCCB Committee on Catholic Education

At the Heart of the Gospel

We need to bring the *Gospel of life* to the heart of every man and woman and to make it penetrate every part of society. This involves above all proclaiming *the core* of this Gospel. It is the proclamation of a living God who is close to us, who calls us to profound communion with himself and awakens in us the certain hope of eternal life. It is the affirmation of the inseparable connection between the person, his life and his bodiliness.

—Blessed John Paul II (EV80–81)

"The flesh is the hinge of salvation." We believe in God who is creator of the flesh; we believe in the Word made flesh in order to redeem the flesh; we believe in the resurrection of the flesh, the fulfillment of both the creation and the redemption of the flesh.

—Catechism of the Catholic Church (1015)

challenges my work has received, seeking to glean as much as possible from what various authors were saying. This book is the fruit of those reflections. I offer it not only for those who have followed the discussion and in the hopes that it will clarify some of the debated points; I offer it also and *even more so* as an invitation to all those involved in the "new evangelization" to reflect on the challenge, hope, and promise that John Paul II's TOB represents for the Church and the world at the beginning of the third millennium.[2]

In light of John Paul II's beatification in May of 2011, we have all the more reason to examine (or re-examine) his "masterwork" and allow its healing rays to penetrate our hearts more deeply. As Monsignor Lorenzo Albacete expressed it in his endorsement of this work: "The beatification of Pope John Paul II is more than the Church's official recognition of his sanctity. John Paul II's teaching is now bequeathed to the Church in a new way—not only by his authority as Pope, but also by his personal experience of sanctity." This book is offered as a celebration of his sanctity and as an invitation to follow in his footsteps. If we do, we cannot help but become ever more effective witnesses to Christ's love in the new evangelization.

At the heart of John Paul II's TOB is the call to love one another in the image of the Trinity, and that means establishing a genuine "unity in diversity." Our differences, even our theological differences, can and should serve to unite us in our common journey towards the fullness of the truth. Very often the resolution of theological debate involves finding the right balance between what appear to be competing truths, but are rather complementary aspects of the whole truth that must be held together in their proper "tension." Finding that proper tension is like tuning a guitar—we inevitably go sharp, then flat, then back again until we find just the right tension in the string. When we understand this, we come to see how we need one another's different emphases. Push-back from either direction is a healthy thing, so long as it's offered charitably, and with a willingness to affirm the truth the "other side" is rightly seeking to uphold.

Dominican author Simon Tugwell observes that our hope in Christ is one of "total integration" in which no truth is lost and "nothing is left hanging." And this, he says, "is why truth can never finally be served or peace proclaimed by taking sides . . . The church is called 'Catholic,' and this means she is committed to saying 'Yes' to the totality of God's truth." He concludes by observing that any "serious and useful undertaking produces a crop of different opinions and schools of thought, and it is from a careful scrutiny of all of them that a man becomes genuinely wise . . . Even the opinions we reject make their own contribution to our vision and understanding" (BSCT, pp. 117-118, 119).

The *Theology of the Body* is the sophisticated work of a mystical theologian. Discovering its gems and absorbing its subtleties is an ongoing process. One never "arrives." There is always more to learn, always more to appreciate, always more to see. Along the way of this journey, the different emphases of various thinkers can only add to our overall understanding, as Father Tugwell expressed. This is why I believe the spirited conversation that the TOB has engendered in recent years represents a positive development and an important catechetical moment for the Church. The signs of the times continue to underscore how desperate is the need—both in and outside the Church—of recovering a vision of the "great mystery" of divine love revealed through our bodies.

With gratitude for all I have gleaned from a host of "different opinions and schools of thought," my goal in this work is simply to unfold what I believe John Paul II, Benedict XVI, and the *Catechism of the Catholic Church* are teaching about this "great mystery" and how we are to share it with the world in the new evangelization. While this work represents a new stage in the development of my own thinking, I also quote from my previous works to show the continuity of my thought and to summarize what I have presented over the years.

It's my sincere hope that all who read this work will enter more deeply into the "great mystery" that lies at the heart of the Gospel and come away all the more compelled to "go into the main streets and invite everyone to the wedding feast" (Mt 22:9).

—Christopher West

Chapter 1

The Great Mystery

"For this reason a man shall leave his father and mother and be joined to his wife, and the two shall become one flesh." This is a great mystery, and I mean in reference to Christ and the Church. (Eph 5:31-32)

At the Heart of the Gospel

At the heart of the Gospel lies the "great mystery" of the marriage of divinity and humanity in the person of Jesus Christ. In the fullness of time, the *two*—God and Man—became *one* in the flesh of the God-Man. Our belief in the Incarnation of God's Son "is the distinctive sign of Christian faith" (CCC 463). It's a mystery so resplendent and grand, so captivating and magnificent, it never ceases to ravish the hearts of those who glimpse its glory. But there's more . . .

As if God's visitation in the flesh weren't enough, this astounding visitation is itself an astounding invitation. At the heart of the Gospel is the God-Man's gratuitous offer to every human being to enter into this same nuptial exchange. God became one in the flesh with us so that we might become one in our flesh with him. "The Word became flesh to make us '*partakers of the divine nature,*'" proclaims the *Catechism of the Catholic Church.* Then, quoting St. Athanasius, the Church boldly declares that "'the Son of God became man so that we might become God'" (CCC 460). Christ humbled himself to share in our humanity so that we might share in his divinity. What a glorious exchange of God and man; what holy nuptials!

Pope Benedict XVI observes that it is man's "primordial aspiration" to "enter into union with God" (DC 10). Yet we rightly intuit that our hearts are too impure to enter so sublime a union. "Go away from me, Lord; I am a sinful man!" (Lk 5:8). As we persevere on our journey with the Lord, we gain confidence to enter the "holy of holies"—the inner sanctuary of union with God—not on our own merits, but only "by the blood of Jesus, by the new and living way which he opened for us through the veil, that is, through his flesh." So let us draw near to this "great mystery," let us enter confidently into these holy nuptials "in full assurance of faith, with our hearts sprinkled clean from an evil conscience and our bodies washed with pure water" (Heb 10:19–20, 22). That is the invitation at the heart of the Gospel.

How do we draw near? How do we enter in? This stupendous mystery is not far away from us. It is not floating in the clouds as an abstract idea. It is very close to us, it is intimately part of us. Indeed, God inscribed this "great mystery" in that deeply felt yearning of our hearts for love and union (what the Greeks called "eros") and signified it in the very form of our bodies when he created us as male and female and called the two to become "one flesh." Right "from the beginning" this call to nuptial union was a foreshadowing of the Word made flesh and his invitation to all humanity to become one with him as members of his body, the Church. As Pope Benedict XVI wrote in a pre-papal essay, understanding the Church as the body of Christ "makes sense only against the backdrop of the formula from Genesis 2:24: 'The two shall become one flesh' (see 1 Cor 6:17). The Church is the body, the flesh of Christ in the spiritual tension of love wherein the spousal mystery of Adam and Eve is consummated" (MCS, p. 26). "For this reason a man shall leave his father and mother and be joined to his wife, and the two shall become one flesh" (Gen 2:24). For what reason? St. Paul tells us in Ephesians 5:31-32—to reveal the "great mystery" of Christ and his love for the Church. The ultimate "reason," the ultimate "logic" of the human body, of the sexual difference, and of spousal union, is to get us in touch with the Ultimate Reason, the Ultimate Logic of the universe: the Logos, the divine Word who has wed himself to our humanity forever.

In Ephesians 5:31-32, St. Paul links the holy communion of spouses and the Holy Communion of Christ and the Church so intimately as to form one "great sacrament," one "great sign" that makes God's invisible mystery visible (see TOB 19:4; 95b:7). We could even say that St. Paul marries these two marriages, that of man and woman and that of Christ and the Church. And this "great mystery" revealed in the marriage of human love and divine love—of eros and agape—is by no means a footnote in the Gospel. Pope John Paul II asserted that "Saint Paul's magnificent synthesis concerning the 'great mystery' appears as the compendium or *summa,* in some sense, *of the teaching about God and man* which was brought to fulfillment by Christ" (LF 19). "It is what God as Creator and Father wishes above all to transmit to mankind in his Word" (TOB 93:2). And God transmits his Word precisely in and through the human body. For "the body, in fact, and only the body, is capable of making visible . . . the mystery hidden from eternity in God" (TOB 19:4). Helping the world to "see" the human body and the "great mystery" of human sexuality in this way is central and essential to the new evangelization.

Reclaiming the Body for the New Evangelization

Catholics believe that popes are chosen not only by the College of Cardinals, but—through them—by the Holy Spirit who is at work to elect a man uniquely suited to address the needs of the Church and the world at that time. When Pope John Paul II was elected to the Chair of Peter in 1978, the Church was facing a dramatic post-conciliar crisis of faith and the world was living under the threat of global destruction by nuclear war. Under such dire circumstances, what might we expect the new pope to offer the Church and the world in his first major teaching project?

John Paul II concluded that one of the most pressing catechetical needs was to help modern men and women understand the meaning of their bodies. Week after week, in a total of 129 Wednesday audience addresses that spanned five years,[3] John Paul II instructed the Church and the world in a thoroughly biblical vision of human embodiment, particularly as it concerns the "great mystery" of our creation as male and female and the call of the two to become "one flesh." The general sense of those in attendance at these theological body-lessons was puzzlement (see WH, p. 333). People expect teachers of the Gospel to emphasize the realm of the spirit. What was all this talk about the body? But this ruptured view of body and spirit was the precise disease John Paul II wanted to remedy. He knew that Christians in the modern world had lost sight of the fact that "at *the core* of this Gospel," as he once put it, "is the affirmation of the inseparable connection between the person, his life and his bodiliness" (EV 81).

No, all of this "talk about the body" was not a distraction from the pope's mission of proclaiming the Gospel to the world. Through this "theology of the body," John Paul II was plunging us anew into "the perspective of the whole gospel, of the whole teaching, of the whole mission of Christ" (TOB 49:3). In the process, he was presenting the Church with an urgent task for the twenty-first century: that of reclaiming the body for the new evangelization. Much is at stake in this task: nothing short of redirecting the "culture of death" from its suicidal course.

"We are facing an immense threat to human life," wrote John Paul II, "not only to the life of individuals, but also to that of civilization itself." We live in "a *society which is sick* and is creating profound distortions in man. Why is this happening?" John Paul asked. "The reason is that our society has broken away from the full truth about man, from the truth about what man and woman really are as persons. Thus it cannot adequately comprehend the real meaning of the gift of persons in marriage, responsible love at the service of fatherhood and motherhood, and the true grandeur of procreation . . . This is the real drama," he concluded, "the modern means of social communication are . . . *falsifying the truth about man.* Human beings are not the same thing as the images proposed by advertising and shown by the modern mass media. *They are much more,* in their physical and [spiritual] unity, as composites of soul and body, as persons. They are much more because of their vocation to love, which introduces them as male and female into the realm of the 'great mystery.'" But the "deep seated roots of the 'great mystery,'" John Paul lamented, "have been lost in the modern way of looking at things. The 'great mystery' is threatened in us and all around us" (LF 19, 20, 21).[4]

Here John Paul II sketched in outline form the war being waged in the modern world over what it means to be human. It's a cosmic contest for man's soul, but the battlefield is the body; the battlefield is man's own vision of himself as male and female, and his understanding of how, as male and female, he is to love.

When Benedict XVI became pope in 2005, the cultural crisis was significantly worse than it was at the time of John Paul II's election in 1978. What was his response? Early in his pontificate, Benedict asserted that his "personal mission" as pope was not to issue many new documents, but to ensure that the teaching of his predecessor was assimilated by the Church (see interview October 16, 2005). Not surprisingly, Pope Benedict's first encyclical, *Deus Caritas Est* (*God is Love*) offered a beautiful continuation—even a crowning—of John Paul II's Theology of the Body. In his own words and with his own style, Pope Benedict reflected at length on the integral relationship between divine love (agape) and the love between the sexes (eros), and how integrating the two is essential if the Church is to be a credible witness in the modern world to the God who "is love."

Building on Benedict XVI's encyclical, in Lent of 2011, Father Raniero Cantalamessa, official preacher to the papal household, offered an illuminating and forthright homily to the pope and the Roman Curia on the urgency of integrating eros and agape. He observed that love "suffers from ill-fated separation not only in the mentality of the secularized world, but also in that of the opposite side, among believers . . . Simplifying the situation to the greatest extent," he said, "we can articulate it thus: In the world we find eros without agape; among believers we often find agape without eros." The former "is a body without a soul" and is well understood "propagated as it is in a hammering way" by the secular media. The latter—agape without eros—"is a soul without a body"; it's a "cold love" in which "the component linked to affectivity and the heart is systematically denied or repressed." Either way, by separating eros and agape, we distort the truth of love and rupture our own humanity. For the "human being is not an angel, that is, a pure spirit; he is a soul and body substantially united: everything he does, including loving, must reflect this structure" (TF I).

The systematic repression of eros in the name of "holiness" ultimately stems from a widespread theological vision of man that splits body and soul in order to "free" love from (what many consider) the "unflattering" and "unholy" realities of bodiliness. Not only is this approach to love terribly flawed, it also conceals within itself a fundamental and grave danger: that of legitimizing and even fostering the world's approach to love. When believers demand a holiness free of eros, the secular world, for its part, quite happily demands an eros free of holiness. Welcome to the world in which we live.

How should the Church respond? Cantalamessa observes that while "we cannot change with one stroke the idea of love that the world has, we can however correct the theological vision that, unwittingly, fosters and legitimizes it" (TF 3). We can and must reclaim the essential link between eros and agape, between sexuality and spirituality, between body and soul. This is the essential cure for what ails the modern world. And this is the essential gift of authentic Catholic teaching on the human body, love, and sexuality, especially as articulated by Popes John Paul II and Benedict XVI.

Defining "Sex" and "Sexuality"

I often tell my audiences the sad (but true) story of a seven-year-old boy who, entering a church for the first time, asked his mother who the man was on the cross. She said, "That's Jesus Christ." To which her son responded, "Mommy, don't say *that,* we're in a church!" How tragic that the most holy, sacred name of Jesus had become for this boy nothing but a bad word! Should his mother stop talking about Jesus, or use some other name to refer to him? Or, rather, should she patiently help rehabilitate her son's thinking? It seems similar today with the words "sex" and "sexuality." The very terms have become vulgar in some people's minds. This makes reclaiming the true holiness of masculinity and femininity and the call of the two to become "one flesh" an obvious challenge in the new evangelization.

Father Cantalamessa observes that the early Christians faced a similar challenge in the original evangelization. Presumably because of its vulgar usage, the New Testament authors avoided the term "eros" altogether. However, as soon as "Christianity entered into contact and dialogue with the Greek culture of the time," writes Cantalamessa, "every preclusion fell immediately." The Fathers of the Church employed a noble usage of eros, and were thus able to rehabilitate an otherwise vulgar word as a "synonym for agape . . . and for every beautiful thing" (TF 3). By following the teachings of the *Catechism,* John Paul II, and Benedict XVI, we can do the same for terms like "sex" and "sexuality."[5]

"*Sexuality* affects all aspects of the human person in the unity of his body and soul," states the *Catechism*. "It especially concerns affectivity, the capacity to love and to procreate, and in a more general way the aptitude for forming bonds of communion with others" (CCC 2332).

"Consequently, sexuality," John Paul II affirmed, "is by no means something purely biological, but concerns the innermost being of the human person as such" (FC 11). A person's "sexuality," therefore (his maleness or femaleness), "in some way is 'constitutive of the person' (not only 'an attribute of the person')" (TOB 10:1).[6] This means our sexuality is not merely one aspect of our humanity. Rather, our sexuality illuminates the very essence of our humanity as men and women made in the divine image.

The more we understand this, the more we recognize how misguided is the common notion that in order to "deny our sinful tendencies" we must "deny our sexuality." With such an approach we end up trading one sin (the lustful indulgence of sexuality) for another (contempt of human nature). When a person denies his sexuality, as Pope Benedict reflected in a pre-papal essay, he "thereby strikes a blow against his deepest being. He holds himself in contempt, because the truth is that he is human only insofar as he is bodily, only insofar as he is man or woman." Hence, the question of sexuality "has high stakes: nothing less than the reality of the creature" (MCS, pp. 32-33). For "every human being is by nature a sexual being," as John Paul II wrote in his pre-papal book *Love and Responsibility*. We are *male* or *female* through and through.[7] And "membership of one of the two sexes means that a person's whole existence has a particular orientation." In turn, this orientation towards the "other"—this "sexual urge"—is not to be understood primarily as an "occasion of sin." Rather, the "sexual *urge* in this conception," writes John Paul II, "is a vector of aspiration along which [our] whole existence develops and perfects itself from within" (LR, pp. 46-47).

Some find themselves markedly uncomfortable identifying our humanity in so close a way with our sexuality. They see it as a reduction of the human person to the "sexual level" and, as such, a debasing or profaning of man's "spiritual dignity." But can we not recognize that dangerous rift between body and soul lurking behind such an idea? It's sin that profanes the great gift of sexuality—original sin and our own personal sin—causing it to descend to a subhuman level. The good news is that Christ has raised the body up again, cleansing our sexuality "by the washing of water with the word" (Eph 5:26). "What God has made clean, [we] are not to call profane" (Acts 11:9).[8] In this light, identifying our humanity so closely with our sexuality is not a matter of reducing the human person to the "sexual level." Rather, it is a matter of *raising all that is sexual to the level of the human person.*

In view of "the redemption of the body" (Rom 8:23), John Paul II's TOB, as George Weigel put it, "challenges us to think of sexuality as a way to grasp the essence of the human—and through that, to discern something about the divine" (WH, p. 343). The "essence of the human" is our call to communion—with God and with one another; it is the giving and receiving of love. And the whole truth of the body and of sex, John Paul affirms, "is the simple and pure truth of communion between persons" (TOB 14:4). This is what makes the sexual realm a profoundly sacred one, and this sacred realm, from the Christian perspective, is the only proper context in which to understand the true nature of sexual matters.

In summary, the terms "sex" and "sexuality," properly understood, refer first and foremost to a rich theological "identity," not to an impersonal or animalistic "activity," as the culture so grossly distorts these words.[9] Only on this indispensable foundation can we speak of the other meaning of the word "sex"—in the sense of the two becoming "one flesh"—without vulgarizing the term as our culture does. Becoming "one flesh" refers "without doubt," John Paul says, to "the unity that is expressed and realized in the conjugal act." But the biblical vision "does not allow us to stop on the surface of human sexuality; it does not allow us to treat the body and sex outside the full dimension of man and the 'communion of persons' [to which he's called in the divine image]." In fact, John Paul says, in discussing sexual matters, we have "the obligation to see the fullness and depth proper to this unity, the unity that man and woman must constitute in the light of the revelation of the body" (TOB 10:2). We must take this obligation very seriously if we are to rehabilitate the terms "sex" and "sexuality" in a noble usage.

Such a noble usage leads to the clear recognition that human sexuality and sexual union in God's design are all about revealing Christ and his love for the Church (see Eph 5:31-32). Indeed, sexual love in God's design is a "great mystery" that takes us to the heart of the Gospel itself. If we are to redirect the culture from its suicidal course, we simply must *re*claim and *pro*claim this sacred truth in a new evangelization.

The Great Task We Face

We "really are in an age in which a new evangelization is needed," asserts Pope Benedict, so that the Gospel message "can reenter our thinking and understanding in a new way" (LW, p. 136). Great numbers of people have been raised and educated in the Church, but "so very little sticks" (LW, p. 140). Why? As the Holy Father admits, the modern crisis in faith stems in part from the fact that the Gospel has been proclaimed "in formulas that, while true, are nevertheless at the same time outmoded. They no longer speak to our living situation and are often no longer comprehensible to us" (LW, p. 63). Hence, we "must seriously reflect on ways to give catechesis a new heart and a new face" (LW, p. 140).

First of all, the "new heart and new face" of catechesis must demonstrate the "positive option" that Christianity provides the world, especially when it comes to questions of sex. Rather than devoting our energies to condemning the world's sin and *accusing* human hearts, we must follow the example John Paul II set in his TOB and focus our efforts on *calling* human hearts to what is true, good, and beautiful (see TOB 44-48). There are, of course, appropriate times to speak about sin and the danger of sin, but that shouldn't be the focus. As Father Jacque Philippe observes: "When we concentrate too much on something that isn't right, and make it our main topic of conversation, we end up giving evil more substance than it has. Deploring evil sometimes only strengthens it . . . We do more to help others experience conversion and make progress by encouraging them in the positive aspects of their lives than by condemning their errors. Good is more real than evil, and it overcomes evil" (IF, pp. 76-77). Benedict XVI confirmed the importance of this approach when he stated:

> Christianity, Catholicism, isn't a collection of prohibitions: it's a positive option. It's very important that we look at it again because this idea has almost completely disappeared today. We've heard so much about what is not allowed that now it's time to say: we have a positive idea to offer, that man and woman are made for each other, that the scale of sexuality, eros, agape, indicates the level of love and it's in this way that marriage develops . . . But [the Church's teaching] is clearer if you say it first in a positive way. (Interview August 5, 2006)

Furthermore, the "new heart and new face" of catechesis must "translate the treasure that is preserved in [our] faith . . . into the speech and thinking of our time," says Pope Benedict, "so that [Christ] can become present within the horizon of the secular world's understanding. That is the great task we face." This great task is under way. However, the pope acknowledges that it "has really not yet succeeded" (LW, p. 64).

Conventional ways of communicating the Catholic Faith have not served us very well in the modern world. Indeed, if we look at how few people in the pews even believe and profess what the Church believes and professes (especially regarding sexual matters)—not to mention those who have left the Church and those who remain un-churched—we must admit that our efforts to evangelize and catechize have not been very successful (to put it mildly). If we really want to reach the men and women of our time with the orthodox teaching of the Church, it will demand something different than what we've seen. First, it will demand, as Pope Paul VI put it, that we "not hold fast to forms of expression which have lost their meaning and can no longer stir men's minds" (ES 85). Second, it will demand, as Blessed John Paul II put it, a proclamation of Christ that is "new in ardor, methods, and expression" (address March 9, 1983). Reaching the modern world with the full truth of the Gospel will demand—if I may put it this way—an "unorthodox" orthodoxy: a vibrant and joyful profession of fidelity to the teaching of the Church proclaimed in a way that breaks out of "outmoded formulas" and speaks to the living situation of the modern world. "For the deposit and the truths of Faith are one thing," observed the Fathers of

Vatican II, "and the manner in which they are enunciated is another" (GS 62).

If Christ is to become present within the secular world's understanding, that will mean walking a fine line, a place of tension, between the sacred and the secular. That will mean, in some instances, using a language with which a more pious and refined audience might take issue so that a much less pious and refined audience might be reached. As Pope Benedict put it, "one has to meet one's listeners halfway, one has to speak to them in terms of their own horizon." We do this not to "stay" there, but "to open up this horizon, to broaden it, and turn our gaze toward the ultimate" (LW, p. 179). Finding that language is a duty of charity. Finding that language is also a process of trial and error. So let us try, and when we err, let us correct those errors and try again. That's how we grow. There's no "one right way" to proclaim the "great mystery" to the modern world, but this much is certain: out of love for others, we must stretch ourselves; we must break out of our comfort zones; we must be courageous, bold, and daring. We must strive to be all things to all men, so that some might be saved (see I Cor 9:22).

Chapter 2

THE WOUND OF PURITANISM

> *We, who live in a country still influenced by puritanism, even if only in reaction against it, have much need to be convinced of the true goodness of our bodies and especially of our own sexuality.*
>
> —Father Paul Quay, S.J. (CMHS, p. 6)

Pope Benedict XVI observes that a hallmark of Christian faith genuinely lived is "the attitude of joy in, and affirmation of the body, of sexuality" that "existed among the first Christians and in the great periods of Christian culture." Living the gift of sexuality in this way, of course, "always requires discipline and responsibility as well," the pope observes. But discipline and responsibility in this realm mustn't be confused with puritanism. "Admittedly," says the Holy Father, "forms of rigorism have also repeatedly gained ground in Christianity, and the tendency toward negative appraisals of sexuality . . . also found its way into the Church." The influence of these distortions has "warped and intimidated people," Benedict XVI forthrightly observes. Thus, it is "evident today that we need to find our way back to the genuinely Christian attitude . . . of joy in, and affirmation of, the body, of sexuality" (LW, p. 103).

This is one of the great gifts of John Paul II's TOB: it enables us to reclaim the joy that genuine Christian cultures have always taken in the body and sexuality. In turn, it serves as a healing balm for those who have been "warped and intimidated" by a negative, fear-based vision of God, the body, and sexuality that has passed for Catholic teaching in many people's minds but *never* has been the authentic vision of the Church. As I wrote in my book *Good News about Sex and Marriage*:

> Christian authors, like many others, have not been exempt from the failure to appreciate fully the goodness and beauty *of* sex. Still, it's important, within the context of this admission, that we not confuse the mind of the Church with the minds of people in the Church. In the face of many attacks, the Church's official teachings have always upheld the inherent goodness of the body and of sexuality. The Church has deemed all contrary systems of thought nothing short of heretical. (GNSM, pp. 38-39)

The Widespread Influence of "Puritanism"

During my presentations over the years, I have asked countless thousands these questions: *How many of you were raised in a Christian home?* Nearly all of my audience raise their hands. Then I ask: *How many of you would say that in your Christian upbringing there was open, honest, normal, healthy conversation about God's glorious plan for making us male and female and calling the two to become one flesh?* Consistently, I get about a 1-2% response. To what do we owe this terrible void? Why didn't anyone tell nearly 99% of the people in the pews about the "great mystery" of their sexuality? Most likely because no one told these people's parents and educators. Why didn't anyone tell them? Most likely because no one told *their* parents and educators. And back the generations it goes.

This deafening and terribly damaging silence about the great gift of our creation as male and female can be traced to widespread cultural attitudes towards the body and sexuality characterized by apprehension, nervousness, discomfort, negativity, fear, suspicion, shame (in the negative sense of the word), etc. Such attitudes are often the fruit of Jansenism, Gnosticism, Manichaeism, or other rigorist heresies condemned by the Church, but the more familiar term to most is "puritanism." We simply cannot understand the history of the sexual revolution—nor, more importantly, can we heal the underlying wound—without understanding how these fearful and negative attitudes have "warped and intimidated people," to quote again from Pope Benedict (LW, p. 103).

Puritanical attitudes inflict deep wounds on the human heart by cutting us off from our deepest identity as men and women made in the divine image. They make us feel like there is something inherently wrong with our creation as bodily, sexual creatures, and that the path to "holiness" is to reject this about ourselves in the name of living a "spiritual" life. This tragically flawed understanding is widespread.[10] When I ask my audience members how many of them grew up thinking of their souls as the "good" or "holy" part of them and their bodies as the "bad" or "unholy" part, the lowest response I've gotten is about 30%, the highest about 90%.

Repression vs. Self-Mastery

When we view our bodies and our sexuality as the base or "less than holy" part of us, we come to conceive of chastity as something essentially negative and repressive. In other words, to quote Karol Wojtyla (the future John

Paul II), we come to conceive of chastity as "a matter of summarily 'annihilating' the value 'body and sex' in the conscious mind by pushing reactions to them down into the subconscious" (LR, p. 171). Wojtyla, on the contrary, sees sensuality—understood here as our spontaneous reactions to the sexual values of others—as the "raw material" of love. Authentic chastity does not repress these reactions, but, with the help of grace, integrates them with and raises them to the level of the dignity of the person. Wojtyla even states that an "exuberant and readily roused sensuality . . . may help the individual to respond more readily and completely to the decisive elements in personal love." And this makes a readily roused sensuality "the stuff from which a rich—if difficult—personal life may be made" (LR, p. 109).

Here, of course, we mustn't confuse repression with self-mastery. While the former stems from and even aggravates the rupture of body and soul, the latter is essential to reintegration and the development of authentic love. Both approaches recognize that, in our fallen world, erotic arousal and emotion typically betray a "utilitarian attitude" towards others, a tendency to *use* others rather than love them. But repression seeks to "manage" this by annihilating erotic arousal and emotion itself—

dominating them in order to "snuff them out." Self-mastery, however, controls "those centers deep within the human being in which the utilitarian attitude is hatched and grows" (LR, p. 170) in order to free erotic arousal and emotion from selfishness and egoism. In turn, as this "control" matures, self-mastery becomes "*the ability to orient* [erotic arousal and emotion] both as to their content and as to their character" (TOB 129:5) in such a way that the true dignity of the person as a "sexual being" is always upheld.

As Wojtyla writes:

> The essence of chastity consists in quickness to affirm the value of the person in every situation, and in raising to the personal level all reactions to the value of "the body and sex." This requires a special interior, spiritual effort [i.e., self-mastery], for affirmation of the value of the person can only be the product of the spirit, but this effort is above all positive and creative "from within," not negative and destructive. It is not a matter of summarily "annihilating" the value "body and sex" [i.e., repression] . . . but of sustained, long-term integration; the value "body and sex" must be grounded and implanted in the value of the person . . . True chastity does

> not lead to disdain for the body . . . That is the result of false chastity, chastity with a tinge of hypocrisy, or, still more frequently, of unchastity. This may be strange and startling—but it cannot be otherwise. (LR, p. 171)

Why might this be strange and startling? Because many people conceive of chastity as a matter of "banishing" the values of the body and sex. But when this approach has been the widespread understanding and practice of "chastity," get ready for a widespread backlash. For it's only a matter of time before what we have "pushed down in to the subconscious" explodes like an overheated pressure cooker. As Wojtyla acknowledged, if chastity "is practiced only in this way, [it] does indeed create the danger of such 'explosions'" (LR, p. 170). This dynamic of repression and explosion gives us keen insight into some of the underlying causes of the sexual revolution, and the life of Hugh Hefner provides an illuminating case study.

Compassion for Sinners

It should cause us pause that the founder of *Playboy* magazine was raised in a Christian home—a Christian home, however, that was steeped in a puritanical approach to the body and sexuality. "Religion was a very important part of my upbringing," explains Hugh Hefner. "I saw in it a quality, in terms of [some] ideals and morality, that I embraced. I also saw part of it, the part related to human sexuality and other things, as hypocritical and hurtful. And I think that is the origin of who I am," says Hefner. "The heart of who I am is a result of trying to make some sense of all of that."[11]

The "sense" he made, of course, was to go from one extreme to the other, launching a pornographic empire that has wrought horrific destruction around the globe. Hefner has made a sixty-year career out of objectifying women and shamelessly encouraging men the world over to follow his lead. In the process he has robbed the innocence of innumerable young people, harmed if not destroyed countless marriages and families, and become one of the main architects of the "culture of death." And behind all the lust and greed can we not recognize something worse still: the pride of our fallen condition that exhibits a " 'love of self even to the point of contempt for God' " (CCC 1850)?

It is right to recognize and disdain these sins. However, we must be careful that our judgment and disdain for the sin does not become—subtly or not so subtly—judgment and disdain for the sinner. For, as the *Catechism* teaches, "although we can judge that an act in itself is a grave offense, we must entrust judgment of persons to the justice and mercy of God" (CCC 1861). Like many people who have been wounded by pornography, I've had to work through a lot of anger and judgment towards people like Hefner. These attitudes may be understandable, but we *must* bring them into the Lord's healing light if we are to grow in genuine love and compassion for the Hugh Hefners of the world, as Christ calls us to do.

One thing that has helped me to grow in compassion has been reading about Hefner's life. His is an extreme case of how people can react when they are "warped and intimidated," as Pope Benedict put it, by negative appraisals of sexuality (see LW, p. 103). From Hefner's account, *Playboy* magazine was his "personal response to the hurt and hypocrisy" of his puritanical upbringing. He elaborates:

> Our family was . . . Puritan in a very real sense . . . Never hugged. Oh, no. There was absolutely no hugging or kissing in my family. There was a point in time when my mother, later in life, apologized to me for not being able to show affection. That was, of course, the way I'd been raised. I said to her, "Mom, . . . because

> of the things you weren't able to do, it set me on a course that changed my life and the world." When I talk about the hurt and hypocrisy in some of our values—our sexual values—it comes from the fact that I didn't get hugged a lot as a kid.[12]

Hefner, of course, cannot simply explain away his behavior as the result of his "not being hugged," nor abdicate responsibility for his evil choices by playing the victim. Such choices, as experience attests, often involve motives dark and hidden. Even so, the above picture of Hefner's life illuminates an important truth.

It's a matter of Catholic theology that when we sin—even grievously—there is some good we are seeking, but we seek it in a disordered way or with a perverse attachment (see CCC 1849). In other words, we're aiming for something good, but like an archer with bad aim, we "miss the mark" (that's what the word "sin" means).

Evil, in fact, as John Paul II wrote, "always, in some way, refers to a good" (SD 7). This means that sin, *The Catholic Encyclopedia* observes, "is not a pure, or entire privation of all moral good" (CE, p. 4). Sin lies in making a choice that involves "a certain lack, limitation, or distortion of good" (SD 7), but the "sinner's intention terminates at some object in which there is [still] a participation of God's goodness," at least to some degree (CE, p. 4).

As Father Simon Tugwell writes,

> Purity of heart makes us sensitive to the good that is truly present even in what is evil. Thus the pseudo-Dionysius [an early Christian mystic], in his chapter on love, reminds us that it is inconceivable that anything or anybody should be totally devoid of good. He takes the example of a sex-maniac. His desire is irrational and wrong; but nevertheless, in so far as what he is looking for is some kind of dim reflection of genuine union and friendship, he has some part in goodness. (BSCT, p. 101)

Hugh Hefner, like the rest of us, is yearning for love and affection. Yet it would seem that, for lack of having his God-given need for love met in healthy, holy ways, he's spent his life trying to meet that need in other ways. That doesn't make his choices any less wrong or any less objectionable, but perhaps it enables us to be more compassionate towards him as a person. "It's the key to my life," says Hefner, "the need to feel loved."[13] "I think I've been searching to fill that hole that was left there in early childhood," he confesses. Regarding his promiscuous lifestyle, he even admits: "I think that what I'm probably doing is avoiding being hurt again. Safety in numbers." Still he laments that, despite countless "lovers," he's "never known a fulfillment of love."[14]

It's impossible, of course, to know a true fulfillment of love apart from the divine plan for love, apart from the God who *is* love. "The desire for God is written in the human heart, because man is created by God and for God . . . Only in God will he find the truth and happiness he never stops searching for" (CCC 27). At his deepest level, whether he knows it or not, Hefner, like every human being, is looking for God, for divine love, for the love revealed and offered in Jesus Christ.

But is the average Christian even capable of introducing someone like Hugh Hefner to the love of Christ in such a way that he could receive it? Hefner himself stated in a 2009 interview that he'd "like to find out what [Jesus Christ] was all about . . . I was raised in a good Methodist home," he said, "and I had questions about organized religion, and I would love to have the answers."[15]

"Seeing" Sinners

If we are to reach "sinners" like Hugh Hefner in the new evangelization, we must first pray for the eyes of the heart to *see* "sinners" like Hugh Hefner. When the "sinful woman" scandalized Simon the Pharisee with her kissing and anointing of Jesus's feet, the Lord looked at her and asked Simon, "Do you see this woman?" (Lk 7:44). The point, of course, is that Simon the Pharisee didn't *see* her. He couldn't, blinded as he was by his indignation.[16]

In my experience, my difficulty *seeing* a "sinner" simply reflects the difficulty I have seeing myself as someone just as desperately in need of mercy as he or she is. We want somehow to remain above those "really bad sinners," to put a safe distance between "us" and "them." But is there really any meaningful difference between "us" and "them"? As Father Tugwell writes:

> We are no more and no less forgivable than anyone else. If we try to privilege our claim to forgiveness, it is not forgiveness we are looking for, but some other kind of recognition. If it is truly forgiveness we are after, then it must be unconditional and unlimited forgiveness. And we

> can receive that only if we are prepared to accept the company that forgiveness places us in. It is no good wanting to be forgiven and then reserving the right to look around disapprovingly on all the other fellows. (BSCT, p. 92)

But there's even more to *seeing* "sinners": it means not only that we recognize their human dignity and what it is they're truly seeking; to *see* "sinners" also means that we are able to recognize Christ in them. As the modern mystic Caryll Houselander put it, even in those who are "dead in their sin," we encounter Christ—Christ in the tomb. Hence, "We should never come to a sinner without the reverence that we would take to the Holy Sepulchre. Pilgrims have traveled on foot for years to kiss the Holy Sepulchre, which is empty. In sinners we can kneel at the tomb in which the dead Christ lies" (RG, pp. 170-171). Oh, if only we were filled with such loving reverence for "sinners"! It is something we must pray for and work towards. The more we receive this gift of reverence for "sinners," the more the apparent difference between "us" and "them" fades. And the more this difference fades, the more we can find common ground on which to agree (see ES 87) and a reference point for entering into meaningful dialogue regarding those issues on which we disagree. Such dialogue leads, as Pope Paul VI wrote, to "the discovery of elements of truth in the opinion of others and makes us want to express our teaching with great fairness" (ES 83). As I wrote in *The Love that Satisfies*:

> You might find this surprising, but we as Catholics actually agree—or *should* agree—with Hugh Hefner's diagnosis of the disease of puritanism. The fear and rejection of the body and sexuality typical of puritanism is laced with a list of interrelated heresies long condemned by the Catholic Church (dualism, gnosticism, spiritualism, Manichaeism, Jansenism, etc.). But if we agree with Hefner's diagnosis of this disease, Christians must disagree with his cure. Hefner's remedy doesn't, in fact, solve the problem of puritanism at all. All he did was flip the puritanical pancake over from repression to indulgence. *Both* approaches flow from the same failure to integrate body and soul, spirituality and sexuality. Only through such an integration can we truly heal the wounds of puritanism. St. Paul called this cure the "redemption of the body" (see Rom 8:23). John Paul II called it living the theology of our bodies. And Benedict XVI calls it the unification of body and soul, *eros* and *agape* [see DC 5-6]. (LS, pp 45-46)

Angelism and Animalism

The *Catechism* takes us to the essence of the healing we need in the following succinct definition of chastity: "Chastity means the successful integration of sexuality within the person and thus the inner unity of man in his bodily and spiritual being" (CCC 2337). Because of the rupture in us caused by original sin, no one is perfectly integrated in this regard. Hence, on the journey towards healing, we tend to lean toward one side of the divide or the other—toward what we might call "angelism" and "animalism." Both contribute equally to the disintegration of man and culture. As I wrote in *Theology of the Body Explained*:

> *Angelism* promotes a "spiritual life" divorced from the body. Failing to uphold the body's personal dignity, it tends toward prudishness and puritanism. Because it considers the body and all things sexual inherently tainted and "unspiritual," it leads to repression of sexual feelings and desire. The angelistic moral code is rigorism; it condemns even some of the most natural manifestations of sexuality as impure. Many Christians throughout history have fallen prey to this distortion. Even today people make

the calamitous mistake of considering this "holiness."

Animalism, on the other hand, springs from a materialistic world view and promotes a "carnal" life divorced from the spirit. Since in this outlook the body and sexual matters are not informed by man's spiritual dignity, animalism tends toward the indecent and the shameless. It encourages men and women to indulge their fallen sexual impulses without restraint and promotes bodily pleasure as man's ultimate fulfillment. The animalistic moral code is permissiveness; it condemns any manifestation of temperance as a hindrance to freedom. All we need to do is turn on the television or walk through the check-out line at a grocery store to see how prevalent this distortion has become.

Cultural trends tend to oscillate between these two extremes. The twentieth century, for example (at least in much of the West), began with a widespread prudishness in which the mere sight of a woman's ankle could cause scandal. Yet it ended with a widespread shamelessness that has "normalized" even the most base sexual perversions. In this way we see how angelism and animalism each contain the seeds of the other.

> There is no "pure" angelist just as there is no "pure" animalist. Each is trying unsuccessfully to suffocate an indomitable aspect of his own nature which, resisting the weight of repression, will eventually explode with a force that propels the person (and the culture) to the other extreme. Pendulum swing is understandable, but the Incarnation teaches another way—the path of (re) integrating spirit and flesh. (TOBE, pp. 40-41)

This is why, after years of oscillating between angelism and animalism, myself, I found John Paul II's TOB so liberating. It showed me a true alternative to the "either-or" of repression and indulgence via the *redemption* of the body, marking the beginning of a true healing in my life.[17]

"Healthy Shame"

It is important to insist that puritanical attitudes are *not* to be confused with a healthy sense of shame (or modesty) which seeks proper reserve in sexual matters and exhibits a healthy desire to veil that which is holy and sacred.[18] As John Paul II states, the need to resist the distorted cultural push to unveil the body (as in pornography) "*is not the effect of a puritanical mentality* or of a *narrow moralism* . . . What is at issue is rather an *extremely important* and fundamental *sphere of values* to which man cannot remain indifferent because of the dignity of humanity" (TOB 62:5). We must foster "healthy customs," as Wojtyla wrote in *Love and Responsibility,* that guard against a shameless exposition of the sexual sphere. However, we must be sure that what we call "healthy customs" has "nothing in common with puritanism in sexual matters. For exaggeration easily results in prudery" (LR, p. 189).

"The human body is not in itself shameful," Wojtyla insisted. "Shamelessness [or immodesty of feeling] is a function of the interior of a person" (LR, p. 191). Thus, there are circumstances in which unveiling the "great mystery" of the body and the sexual sphere is not irreverent or immodest. "If someone takes advantage of such an occasion . . . it is only he who is guilty of shamelessness (immodesty of feeling), not the other" (LR, p. 190). For example, if someone walks into the Sistine Chapel and looks upon Michelangelo's nudes as an opportunity to indulge his lusts, it is he who is guilty of shamelessness, not Michelangelo. In fact, in the case of the Sistine Chapel, we find an example of John Paul II himself correcting an unhealthy exaggeration of the principle of "veiling." As part of the restoration project of the famed chapel, John Paul II ordered the removal of many of the loincloths that previous churchmen had ordered to cover Michelangelo's original nudes.[19] He even described the restored Sistine Chapel with its newly unveiled figures as "*the sanctuary of the theology of the human body.*" For it seemed to John Paul II "that Michelangelo, in his own way, allowed himself to be guided by the evocative words of the Book of Genesis which . . . reveals: 'The man and his wife were both naked, yet felt no shame (Gen 2:25)" (*L'Osservatore Romano,* April 13, 1994). Hence, as Pope Benedict observed, "the bodies of Michelangelo are inhabited by light, life, splendor" (address May 13, 2011).

The point is this: while there are certainly circumstances that call for veiling the body and the sexual sphere that cannot be confused with a puritanical mentality, there are also circumstances that call for a careful and respectful "lifting of the veil" in order to correct a puritanical mentality that cannot be confused with irreverence or shamelessness. Quoting again from Father Simon Tugwell, chastity not only requires us to revolt against sexual license; "Christian chastity, too, requires a revolt against Victorian prudishness. The Church is not just there to sacralize primness" (BSCT, p. 126).

Both veiling and unveiling are Scriptural themes of significance to this discussion (e.g., see Ex 26:31-33; 2 Cor 3:13-18; Mk 15:38; Heb 6:19, 10:19-20). Indeed, the "tearing of the temple veil" from "top to bottom" at the moment of Christ's death (see Mk 15:38) is a mystery of unfathomable depths. "In the liturgy, the curtain between heaven and earth is torn open" (SL, p. 125), and Christ invites us to *enter in* with confidence and full assurance of faith that we are welcome here. We can now enter behind the veil—not because of our own merit, but because of what Christ has done for us. "Therefore, brothers and sisters, since we have confidence to enter the sanctuary by the blood of Jesus, by the new and living way which he opened for us through the veil . . . let us draw near with a true heart in full assurance of faith, with our hearts sprinkled clean from an evil conscience and our bodies washed with pure water" (Heb 10:19-20).

All conversations about "veiling" must be balanced with the truth that Christ himself has removed the veil and he bids us to enter the mystery with "hearts sprinkled clean." An overemphasis on veiling coupled with an overly cautious attitude towards unveiling can effectively "take away the key to knowledge," as Jesus put it. Those locked in this imbalance do not enter the mystery themselves, and they often "hinder those who are trying to enter" (see Lk 11:52).

A Delicate Balance

The proper balance here between veiling and "lifting the veil" is a delicate one, and it lies in the tension of the following paradox. An orthodox presentation of human sexuality must be the presentation of a "great mystery" (Eph 5:31-32) that is somehow revealed (which means "unveiled") while honoring the veil; it must somehow be revealed without ceasing to be a mystery that remains "hidden."

Here we encounter one of those Catholic "both-and" realities: veiled and unveiled at the same time? How is that possible? We almost inevitably seek to resolve the tension by leaning towards one side or the other. As John Paul II wrote, in the history of man's evaluation of his own body and sexuality, "he passes from the pole of pessimism to the pole of optimism, from puritanical strictness to present-day permissiveness" (TOB 44:4). So—inevitably—there will be some who, in seeking rightly to veil the mystery, go too far, leaning towards prudery. And—inevitably—there will be others who, in seeking rightly to reveal the mystery, go too far, leaning towards "crudery," shall we say. Both are trying to uphold an important truth but are failing to balance it with another important truth.

Is it even possible to strike such a delicate balance? What would it look like? I believe we can see a beautiful example of this in the Song of Songs. Here we have an unabashed biblical revelation (revelation, again, means "unveiling") of erotic love, but one that, through the poetic use of metaphors, creatively honors the veil. "The language of metaphors—poetic language—seems to be especially appropriate and precise in this sphere," observes John Paul II (TOB 110:8). Such language enables us to reflect on profoundly intimate, sensual, and erotic matters without spoiling or profaning them. "For in this book," as Pope St. Gregory the Great observed, "kisses are mentioned, breasts are mentioned, cheeks are mentioned, loins are mentioned." These words paint "holy pictures" which "are not meant for mockery or laughter." Rather, they are meant "to incite us to a holy loving." In the erotic poetry of the Song, while God "lowers himself in words, he also elevates our understanding; for from the words associated with this sensual love we learn how fiercely we are to burn with love for the Divine" (see TSS, p. 8).

Seeking Integration and Healing

Blessed John Henry Newman asserts that the object of a Catholic education "is to reunite things which were in the beginning joined together by God and have been put asunder by man" (SP, sermon I). We are all disintegrated creatures in need of healing. No one can claim to live in perfect balance here. In order to work towards that balance, it can be a fruitful exercise to reflect on our own leanings.

In the issue under discussion, we should ask ourselves: Do I tend to revolt against sexual license while downplaying the revolt against prudishness? Or do I tend to revolt against prudishness while downplaying the revolt against license? Do I find myself uncomfortable with the nude and semi-nude art in St. Peter's Basilica and the Sistine Chapel? If so, why? Or, on the other hand, do I find myself uncomfortable with the fact that the Vatican also strictly enforces a dress code in order to enter St. Peter's Basilica and the Sistine Chapel? If so, why?

Whatever direction we may lean, we can be sure to find a certain "push-back" coming from those who lean the other way. This kind of push-back is understandable and even healthy in our search for the proper balance between what appear to be "competing truths." But sometimes such push-back can escalate into an unhealthy and vitriolic polarization. To the extent that we harden our own positions and refuse to affirm the truth the other is trying to uphold, we only aggravate the rift and deepen the wound. The way to overcome polarization, then, is for those on different sides of a question to humble themselves and acknowledge the truth that the other side seeks to uphold.

Those who emphasize the need to veil the sacred mystery of sexuality make an entirely valid point. And even if, in some cases, that point is taken too far and exhibits a certain overly cautious attitude, I think that's understandable in an environment where a pornographic stripping of the body is so prevalent. It needs to be balanced out by a proper sense of "revelation," but it's understandable. Similarly, those who emphasize the Christian "revelation" of the body make an entirely valid point. And even if, in some cases, their point is taken too far, I think that's understandable in an environment where puritanical attitudes have held sway. It needs to be balanced out by a proper sense of reserve and veiling, but it's understandable.

And so we can see here how those with different emphases need one another. For no single person has the complete picture. When we rely on the gifts and insights of others to make up what is lacking in our own, that's simply the body of Christ being itself. And when the body of Christ is being itself, when we find that place of proper tension and balance, we're sure to encounter a responsible and joyful approach to sexuality such as "existed among the first Christians and in the great periods of Christian culture" (LW, p. 103).

Chapter 3

THE SACRAMENTALITY OF THE BODY

The body in its masculinity and femininity has been called "from the beginning" to become the manifestation of the spirit. The body, in fact, and only the body, is capable of making visible what is invisible: the spiritual and the divine.

—John Paul II (TOB 45:2; 19:4)

I would contend that, theologically speaking, there is no greater scandal, no greater affront to typical human "sensibilities," than the Christian claim that the Supreme and Ultimate Being, the Infinite and Ineffable Source of all that exists—God—took on a human body in the womb of a young woman from Nazareth. A God with hair and fingernails!? A God with a stomach, lungs, and a beating heart!? A God who was, as St. Augustine put it, "complete in all the parts of a man" (*City of God* XXII .18)? The fact that God communicates his divine mystery through human flesh never fails to rankle the mind and confound the human heart. Even many Christians, while they may accept the Incarnation in theory, find the implications of an enfleshed God too much to bear.

As Caryll Houselander wrote, "those who accept revelation on this matter do not always accept it altogether: their intellects [may] accept it, but emotionally they do not accept it at all." For many, she says, having to accept the Church's teaching on the Incarnation "is rather like having to accept an old hat from our grandmother, who will leave us a fortune so long as we respect her old hat. The idea of wearing the old hat [however] is out of the question." They revolt, Houselander concludes, because they happen to find the flesh "shocking." They want instead to "get away from the flesh . . . and live what they call a 'spiritual life' " (RG, pp. 91-92). Indeed, they cannot seem to accept that God who is pure Spirit has lowered himself to the level of "flesh" in order to raise our flesh up. They seem to pit the "material" against the "spiritual," the "lower" against the "higher," the "visible" against the "invisible," the "body" against the "divine." But this betrays a failure to enter the "great mystery" at the heart of the Gospel.

The Logic of the Logos Made Flesh

As Benedict XVI explained in his pre-papal book *The Spirit of the Liturgy*, "The Incarnation means, in the first place, that the invisible God enters into the visible world, so that we, who are bound to matter, can know him." And "this descent of God is intended to draw us into a movement of ascent" (SL, pp. 122-123). It is precisely because God has made this "descent into the flesh" that all of material reality has been "infused" in some way with traces of the divine presence, and this applies most especially to the human body. This is what allows us to seek understanding of the "higher" *in* the "lower." He's there! He's come among us *in the flesh*! Through the Incarnation, we are able, Benedict XVI observes, "to grasp the Whole in the fragment, the Infinite in the finite, God in the history of humanity" (Address to Artists, November 21, 2009).

We are "bound to matter" as human beings. We not only *need not* "skip over" the lower to reach the higher; we *cannot*. As the *Catechism* states, "We can name God only by taking creatures as our starting point" (CCC 40). In our futile attempts to "skip over" the created order to reach God, what appears as liberation from what some consider the "unpleasantries" of the material world ends in the denial of everything the Incarnation steadfastly affirms. Ironically, by fleeing the material world in search of the spirit, we actually embrace the essential tenet of materialism: "matter is absolutized," as Pope Benedict points out, "and thought of as completely impervious to God, as mere matter, and thus deprived of its dignity" (SL, p. 124). The Christian response to materialism, therefore, is not "spiritualism." That's just the flip side of the same terribly flawed coin. The Christian response to both materialism and spiritualism is the *Incarnation,* it is *Christ*: Word made flesh; God embodied. Oh!—how blessed is the flesh that gave him flesh! How blessed is the womb that bore him and the breasts that he sucked! (see Lk 11:27).

The *Incarnational* view of reality—the authentically Christian view—recognizes that, for man, there is no reaching the "higher" without pondering the "lower." In understanding the "lower" *theologically,* we reach the "higher" precisely because the "higher" has descended into the "lower," penetrating its very DNA. This is the logic of *the* Logic (the *Logos*) taking on flesh.

Hans Urs von Balthasar writes of this logic as follows: "We cannot look directly at Christ any more than we can look directly at the sun. He has to be 'interpreted'" (GW, p. 57). And the Incarnation—God revealed in the flesh—is this "interpretation." As Balthasar says, Christ's "works, words, miracles are one and all signs that point to something . . . They possess an unbounded depth into which they attract and invite us." This "unbounded depth" is the infinite spiritual reality behind the physical signs of Christ's Incarnate life. However, as Balthasar observes—and this is the key point—"we do not find the truth behind [these physical signs] at a second, purely spiritual level . . . Rather (and the Fathers affirmed this as well): the Word became Flesh, the eternal Meaning has become incarnate within the temporal symbol. What is signified must be sought within the sign itself . . . the God within the Man. No one shall ever leave Christ's humanity behind as an obsolete instrument" (GW, p. 57).

In short, we needn't ask forgiveness of the body. In virtue of the Incarnation, material reality *does* provide a key to spiritual things. In virtue of the Incarnation we have the right (and the duty!) to look for understanding of the "higher" *in* the "lower." Conversely, as John Paul II states, repeating here the teaching of L. Alonso-Schokel, "he who must ask forgiveness of the body, does not have the right to rise higher" (TOB 108:1, note 96). "God took on the body, he revealed himself in it," Pope Benedict observes. We witness here "the humble movement of God who lowers himself toward the body to then raise it up to himself." Redeemed in Christ, the human body "becomes ever more full of light and of the Spirit, full of God. Here," Pope Benedict concludes, "appears the profundity of the theology of the body" (address May 13, 2011).

John Paul II's Thesis

The very phrase "theology of the body" indicates John Paul II's working principle: he's pondering the mystery of the human body in order to reach theological truths. Yes, he is pondering the human body to find answers to questions "of the spirit" revealed. As I once heard it stated quite succinctly, if the language of Israel is Hebrew and the language of Islam is Arabic, the language of Christianity is *the body*. For, as John Paul II makes clear: "The body, in fact, and only the body, is capable of making visible what is invisible: the spiritual and the divine. It has been created to transfer into the visible reality of the world the mystery hidden from eternity in God, and thus to be a sign of it" (TOB 19:4).

This is not an obscure footnote in the TOB. It is the pope's essential thesis statement, the brush with which he paints his entire catechesis. We who have been raised with "materialism" on the one hand and "spiritualism" on the other must say it again and again until it sinks in and transforms us: *We needn't flee from the flesh or the material world to encounter the spirit*! The marriage of flesh and spirit lies at the heart of the Gospel and at the heart of our humanity.

As the *Catechism* relates: "As a being at once body and spirit, man expresses and perceives spiritual realities through physical signs and symbols." This is not a handicap we must try to overcome. This is part of our nature that we must welcome and embrace. "As a social being, man needs signs and symbols to communicate with others . . . The same holds true for his relationship with God" (CCC 1146). And the fundamental sign we "need"—the fundamental sign through which God communicates himself to us—is the human body. This is the very *purpose* of the body "from the beginning"; this is the body's native "language"—to proclaim mysteries of a spiritual and divine nature. The body's ability to do so flows from the very sacramentality of creation.

The Sacramentality of Creation

"Even before revealing himself to man in words of truth, God reveals himself to him through the universal language of creation" (CCC 2500). "All creatures bear a certain resemblance to God, most especially man . . . Consequently we can name God by taking his creatures' perfections as our starting point, 'for from the greatness and beauty of created things comes a corresponding perception of their Creator'" (CCC 41). This means that all of creation is "sacramental" inasmuch as it reveals something of spiritual and divine reality. "The heavens declare the glory of God; the skies proclaim the work of his hands . . . Their voice goes out into all the earth" (Ps 19:1-4). For ever "since the creation of the world his invisible nature, namely, his eternal power and deity, has been clearly perceived in the things that have been made" (Rom 1:20). And we as bodily, sexual beings are the crown of all he has made. This means our incarnate humanity as male and female reveals the divine mystery more than anything else in the created order. For we are made "male and female" in the divine image. Indeed, to say "theology of the body" is just another way of saying we're "made in the image of God."

St. Bonaventure expressed these truths this way:

> The creatures of the sense world signify *the invisible attributes of God* . . . For every creature is by its nature a kind of effigy and likeness of eternal

> Wisdom, but especially one that in the book of scripture has been elevated through the spirit of prophecy to prefigure spiritual things; and most especially, those creatures . . . which God willed to institute as a symbol and which has the character not only of a sign in the general sense but also of a sacrament. (ACM, p. 241)

Making visible the invisible is what John Paul II means by speaking of the sacrament, or "sacramentality," of the body. "The body in its masculinity and femininity has been called 'from the beginning' to become the manifestation of the spirit. It becomes such a manifestation also through the conjugal union of man and woman when they unite with each other so as to form 'one flesh.'" Through this unity, "the body in its masculinity and femininity [i.e., its sexuality] takes on the value of a sign, in a certain sense a sacramental sign" (TOB 45:2). It is "a *sign that* efficaciously *transmits in the visible world the invisible mystery hidden in God from eternity*" (TOB 19:4).

What is this "mystery hidden in God from eternity" (see Eph 3:9) of which the body is a sign? And in what way is the body a sign of it? These are sublime questions. As I wrote in *Theology of the Body Explained,* "Lest we proceed too quickly or casually, we should remember that angels fear to tread where John Paul II humbly dares to take us. His entire catechesis offers patient, prayerful, and studied reflections on these two questions—always with profound reverence for the transcendent 'otherness' of the Mystery he is pondering" (TOBE, pp. 17-18). Here are some initial considerations, however, as to the manner in which we can look to the human body to find answers to questions "of the spirit" revealed:

> The divine mystery is invisible, intangible, incommunicable, ineffable. It is so vast, so far "beyond" man that the only way one can possibly encounter it is if the Mystery chooses to come down to our level and reveal itself. The Mystery *has.* This is the Church's astounding claim and proposal to the world. "By sending his only Son and the Spirit of Love in the fullness of time, God has revealed his innermost secret: God himself is an eternal exchange of love, Father, Son, and Holy Spirit, and he has destined us to share in that exchange" (CCC 221) . . . If we listen carefully and prayerfully to what the body "says," we will come to hear it whispering to us [that] God is an eternal communion of love and we are destined to share in this divine bliss! It is *this* theological reality that the human body signifies.

But what enables us to understand the body in this way? According to John Paul's catechesis, it is precisely the gratuitous beauty of sexual difference and the call of man and woman to become "one flesh" (Gen 2:24). "The sacrament, as a visible sign, is constituted with man," the Pope says, "through his 'visible' masculinity and femininity" (TOB 19:4). In this sacramental context "we fully understand the words in Genesis 2:24 . . . : 'For this reason a man will leave his father and his mother and unite with his wife, and the two will be one flesh'" (TOB 19:5). In other words, spousal union in God's design is the original effective sign that communicates the "great mystery" of the inner life of the Trinity to the world. *Stunning.* The more we ponder this, the more the implications multiply. To begin with, the body—and more specifically, the union of man and woman in "one flesh"—*must* be essentially linked to the Incarnation of the Word. For Christ, and *only Christ,* can communicate divine life to the world. Indeed: as St. Paul says, the one flesh union is a "great mystery," a great foreshadowing that *refers to Christ and the Church* (see Eph 5:31–32). And it does so right from the beginning!

In short, . . . human sexuality "is an echo in the human creature," as Angelo Cardinal Scola expresses it, "of that unfathomable mystery from which Jesus Christ has lifted a corner of the veil: the difference in perfect unity that exists in the Trinity, the three persons who are the one God." Scola concludes that the "most appropriate word, coined by Christian thought, for indicating this impenetrable mystery is 'communion'" (NM, p. 131). God himself is an eternal *Communion* of three Persons. This is the "theology" inscribed in the human body, in masculinity and femininity. A man's body does not make sense by itself, nor does a woman's body. Seen in light of each other, we discover the call to *communion.* And this communion of "two," in the normal course of events, leads to "a third" (see TOB 21:4).

Here we discover an earthly sign, a created or human version, so to speak, of the Uncreated divine mystery of the Trinity. "In some way, therefore—even if in the most general way—the body enters into the definition of sacrament, which is 'a visible sign of an invisible reality,' namely, of the spiritual, transcendent, and divine reality. In this sign—and through this sign—God gives himself to man in his transcendent truth and in his love" (TOB 87:5). (TOBE, pp. 18-19)

Of course we can't reduce the spiritual and divine mystery to its bodily sign. The Mystery itself *infinitely* transcends its bodily sign. Thus, the body never affords a total clearing of the mystery it signifies (see TOBE, pp. 19-20).

Two Fundamental Progressions

With this teaching on the "sacramentality of the body," John Paul II, in keeping with the Second Vatican Council, wants to correct a widespread current of thought that fails to recognize the link that Christ established between theology (the study of God) and anthropology (the study of man). John Paul observes in one of his early encyclicals that many currents of thought both in the past and today tend to separate theology and anthropology and even set them in opposition. The Church, however, "seeks to link them up in human history in a deep and organic way." In fact, the Holy Father states that an emphasis on this theology-anthropology link was "one of the basic principles, perhaps the most important one, of the teaching of the [Second Vatican] Council" (DM 1).

Precisely because of this deep, organic link between theology and anthropology, Fathers Hogan and LeVoir observe that "in the Holy Father's thought, there can be found two fundamental progressions: one beginning with man and moving to God, and the other beginning with God and moving to man. Obviously, Christology, the study of the God-man, is at the center of both these movements" (CL, p. 36). Quoting from my TOB commentary:

> The whole of John Paul II's theological and anthropological vision flows . . . from the Father, through Christ's spousal love for the Church and into the lives and bodies of concrete men and women . . . [But] we can also move in the other direction—from the human body to the union of the sexes, from there to the union of Christ and the Church, and from there to the union of the three Persons of the Trinity. This is obviously not a "continuum." For an infinite abyss separates the creature from the Creator. We can only cross that abyss from earth to heaven because Christ himself first crossed it from heaven to earth. Once again, we see that everything in the TOB hinges on the Incarnation. (TOBE, p. 35)

An integral "theology of the body," therefore, is not just a view of the body from God's perspective (a descending view). It is also a "view of God," shall we say, from the body's perspective (an ascending view). Failure to hold these two progressions together leads both to erroneous concepts of God and to erroneous concepts of our bodies. God becomes an unreachable phantom and the body becomes a merely physical, biological reality.

The Cartesian Split

In my experience speaking to audiences around the world, very few Christians understand their bodies as something *theological.* Indeed the very phrase "theology of the body" strikes most people as a strange contradiction in terms. But this only serves to demonstrate how deep-seated the Cartesian worldview—that modern split between body and soul that began with René Descartes' dictum: "I think therefore I am"—has become and how far we have drifted from an authentically Christian, incarnational, sacramental vision of the real. By pondering the Christian mystery—the mystery of the Incarnation—we discover that the *theological* and *bodily* realms not only belong together, they are, in fact, "destined" for each other. As St. Paul put it, the body is *meant* for the Lord, and the Lord is *meant* for the body (see I Cor 6:13). If it seems strange to see "theology" in our bodies, it shouldn't if we take the truth about Christmas to its logical conclusions. As John Paul II put it, "Through the fact that the Word of God became flesh, the body entered theology . . . through the main door" (TOB 23:4).

As I wrote in my TOB commentary, "the TOB is not only a response to the sexual revolution, it's a response to the Enlightenment. It's a response to modern rationalism, Cartesian dualism, and all the disembodied anthropologies infecting the modern world" (TOBE, p. 14). As Christians, we must have the courage to make an honest and thorough self-assessment to see where these disembodied views may have affected our own sentiments, perspectives, and language. For most of us who have grown up in the Western world, modern rationalism—that Cartesian view of man that reduces him to a "thinking thing" housed in human flesh—has simply been the predominant lens presented to us through which to view the world. But it is a terribly jaded lens that effectively blinds us to the theology of our bodies. And, precisely because of such blindness, we are unable to see how the "lower" reality of the body reveals the "higher" reality of the spirit and the divine (see TOB 19:4). As Peter Kreeft writes:

Pre-Cartesian cultures did not divide reality into two mutually exclusive categories of purely immaterial spirit and purely nonspiritual matter. Rather, they saw all matter as in-formed, in-breathed by spirit . . . This vision applied especially to . . . the human body, nature's masterpiece and microcosm. We manifest the materiality of spirit as well as the spirituality of matter; in us, spirit is made incarnate. The human spirit is the soul *of the body*; it is not just temporarily juxtaposed with it, like a ghost in a machine, or a sardine in a can, or a prisoner in a cell (though this Platonic view persisted as an influential heresy alongside Christian orthodoxy and is perennially confused with it) . . .

Descartes initiates "angelism" when he says, "My whole essence is in thought alone." Matter and spirit now become "two clear and distinct ideas." . . . This is *our* common sense; we have inherited these categories, like nonremovable contact lenses, from Descartes, and it is impossible for us to understand pre-Cartesian thinkers while we wear them. Thus we are constantly reading our modern categories anachronistically into the authors of the Bible. (EKH, pp. 86-87)

The Spirit Affirms the Body

An index of our "Cartesian assumptions," Kreeft goes on to observe, is our puzzlement over Pauline terms such as the "spiritual body" (1 Cor 15:44). Or, we could also point to the difficulty many people have with the phrase "theology of the body." Both of these notions are "a pure contradiction in terms, Cartesianly speaking" (EKH, p. 89). Another such index would be the typical belief that "living by the Spirit" means rejecting our bodies, for "the desires of the Spirit are against the flesh" (Gal 5:17). But the "flesh" of which Paul speaks is not a Cartesian "body." It is the whole person (body and soul) cut off from God's inspiration. "It is the 'man of concupiscence,' that is, the man of disordered desire" (see TOB 51:1). To live "by the Spirit" means we open our entire humanity (body and soul) to the indwelling of the Spirit, and in this way our "mortal bodies" are also infused with life "through his Spirit" (Rom 8:11). What then are we to make of Jesus' statement that "the flesh is of no avail"? John Paul II responds: "In spite of appearances, these words ['It is the spirit that gives life, the flesh is of no avail,' from John 6:63] express the highest affirmation of man—the affirmation of the body given life by the Spirit" (RH 18).

As we allow these truths to peel away the Cartesian lenses glued to our pupils, we come to see the whole world differently. We no longer view the physical world primarily as a "dangerous" place against which we must constantly be on guard. We no longer think of the "lower" as an obstacle to the "higher." Rather, the more we enter into union with God and his vision, we see all of creation as a springboard that leads to the very Mystery of the divine, and we rejoice in it. "Creation, and other people in particular," John Paul tells us, "not only regain their true light, given to them by God the Creator, but, so to speak, they lead us to God himself, in the way that he willed to reveal himself to us: as Father, Redeemer, and Spouse" (MI, p. 30).

The key point in all of this is that we must carefully guard our minds and hearts against any tendency of thought or attitude that separates body and soul or sets body and spirit (the "lower" and the "higher") in fundamental opposition. There is a "tension" here for sure, a "disposition of powers," as John Paul II observes, at war between body and spirit. But this is only the result of original sin (see TOB 51:1). "In the beginning it was not so." Peace in this war is *never* to be found by separating ourselves from our bodies. It is literally *impossible* to separate one's "self" from one's body. The soul is not the self. As St. Thomas Aquinas stated: "my soul is not me."[20] Professor John Saward observes that the "soul on its own can no more be called a person than a hand or a foot on its own" (RW, p. 16).

There is a word we use to describe the separation of body and soul—*death*. If a person is trying to live a "spiritual" life divorced from his body, such a person is "dead." He does not know who he is or who he is called to be.[21] But here's the good news: even if we are "dead," even if we've been "cut off" from our bodies our whole lives because of a faulty vision of our humanity, we can be raised to new life again. "If the Spirit of him who raised Jesus from the dead dwells in you, he who raised Christ Jesus from the dead will give life to your mortal bodies also through his Spirit who dwells in you" (Rom 8:11). And we must insist with John Paul II that this "redemption of the body" is not only something we wait for at the end of time. Certainly, the fullness of this redemption will only come with the eschaton, the final reality at the end of time. But "*the 'redemption of the body' is already an aspect of human life on earth.* This redemption is not just an eschatological reality but a historical one as well. It shapes the history of the salvation of concrete living people" (PC, p. 326).

The Church's Reply to the Cartesian Split

In summary of this chapter, we must recognize that since God has revealed his mystery through the Word made flesh, he wants us to look to that flesh, our flesh—for it is "our flesh" that he took on—to find him there. "Blessed are the pure in heart, for they shall see God" (Mt 5:8). This is the "great mystery" that lies at the heart of the Gospel: the discovery of God in the body. And this is why, in its course, John Paul II's TOB plunges us into "the perspective of the whole gospel, of the whole teaching, even more, of the whole mission of Christ" (TOB 49:3).

In short, the TOB is one of the Church's most critical efforts in modern times to help the world become more "conscious of the mystery and reality of the Incarnation" (TOB 23:4)—and, through that, to become more conscious of the very purpose and meaning of human life. The Second Vatican Council, in one of its most important statements, put it this way: "The truth is that only in the mystery of the incarnate Word does the mystery of man take on light. For Adam, the first man, was a figure of him who was to come, namely Christ the Lord. Christ, the final Adam, by the revelation of the mystery of the Father and his love, fully reveals man to himself and makes his supreme calling clear" (GS 22). This bold proclamation became John Paul II's anthem. In fact, he considered it "the reply, so long awaited, which the Church has given to modern rationalism" (LF 19)—to that horrific rift between spirit and matter initiated by Descartes' dualistic view of man.

How does Christ reveal "the mystery of the Father and his love" and thus "fully reveal man to himself"? Precisely through *his body*. For the "body, in fact, and only the body, is capable of making visible what is invisible: the spiritual and the divine" (TOB 19:4). The body and only the body is capable of revealing "the mystery of the Father and his love." Thus, the body and only the body "fully reveals man to himself and makes his supreme calling clear." What is that supreme calling? Mystical marriage . . . with God . . . experienced also with the whole communion of saints. This is the "higher" reality to which the "lower" leads because of that mysterious principle of "Incarnation" that links theology and anthropology, God and the body. Whatever our particular fears or reluctance, John Paul insists that "we must act upon this principle with faith, with an open mind and with all our heart" (DM 1).

Chapter 4

The Transformation of Desire

For the mind of the one who is continually with God even his concupiscence abounds beyond measure into a divine desire and his entire irascible element is transformed into divine love. For by an enduring participation in the divine illumination, it becomes altogether shining bright . . . changed over from earthly things to divine.

—Saint Maximus the Confessor (ACM, p. 129)

This quote from St. Maximus takes us to the heart of one of John Paul II's most important (and most controversial) teachings: the power of Christ's death and resurrection to transform our desires by liberating our hearts from the domination of concupiscence. Although it's not a term used in everyday language, we all know the experience of concupiscence, that disordering of our passions caused by original sin. When we feel the desire to eat more than we should, that's concupiscence. When we feel a desire to grasp at riches and power, or to boost our own ego, that's concupiscence. When we feel that pull within our hearts to treat another person merely as an object of emotional or physical gratification, that's concupiscence. Concupiscence is simply a fact of our fallen condition. However, while it comes from sin and inclines us to sin, concupiscence is not itself a sin (see CCC 2515). It cannot harm those who do not consent to it (see CCC 1264).

As we can see, concupiscence refers to more than sexual lust. St. John speaks of a "threefold concupiscence" in his first letter: "For all that is in the world, the concupiscence of the flesh and the concupiscence of the eyes and the pride of life, is not of the Father, but is of the world. And the world passes away, and the concupiscence thereof; but he who does the will of God abides forever" (1 Jn 2:16-17). What *is* the "will of God" in this regard? And what is man really capable of in his battle with concupiscence?

John Paul II explores these questions at great length in his reflections on Christ's words from the Sermon on the Mount about looking "lustfully" (see Mt 5:27-28). By describing such a look as adultery in the "heart," Christ is not condemning the body or our God-given attraction to the body. Rather, as John Paul II states, Christ is calling us "to overcome the threefold concupiscence and in particular the concupiscence of the flesh" (TOB 46:1). But is it really possible to "overcome concupiscence"? This is a particularly important question. In a very real way it takes us to the heart of the Gospel itself. "This is what is at stake," John Paul II maintained, "the *reality* of Christ's redemption. *Christ has redeemed us!* This means he has given us the possibility of realizing the *entire truth* of our being; he has set our freedom free from the *domination* of concupiscence" (VS 103).

The Condition of All Life Together in the Truth

Some authors, even some well respected theologians, seem to believe that concupiscence is insurmountable.[22] It is true, as John Paul II says, that when man leaves his heart "*at the mercy of the forces of nature he cannot avoid the influence of the concupiscence of the flesh*" (TOB 46:3). That said, man is not simply at the mercy of the forces of nature. "It is important," John Paul states, "that precisely in his 'heart' [man] does not feel himself irrevocably accused and given up to the concupiscence of the flesh, but that in the same heart he feels himself called with energy [to the] supreme value, which is love" (TOB 46:6). Through the mystery of *the redemption of the body,* man is "called with effectiveness," John Paul says, "*to rediscover,* or even better, to realize, the spousal meaning of the body" (TOB 46:4), which refers to the body's *"power to express love: precisely that love in which the human person becomes a gift* and—through this gift—fulfills the very meaning of his being and existence" (TOB 15:1).

In fact, as John Paul II sees it, liberation of the heart from concupiscence "is the condition of all life together in truth." For without this liberation, we are not free to be a gift to one another (see TOB 43:6). Or, shall we say, when the heart is dominated by concupiscence, we lose the "sincerity" of the gift. And, as Vatican II proclaimed and John Paul incessantly repeated, "man can only find himself through the sincere gift of self" (GS 24).

As the *Catechism* points out, the idea that concupiscence is "insurmountable" actually flows from the Protestant Reformation's view that original sin "radically perverted man and destroyed his freedom" (see CCC 406). The Catholic position is that original sin wounded man terribly "but human nature has not been totally corrupted." While it's certainly true that even after Baptism, "the consequences for nature, weakened and inclined to evil, persist in man and summon him to spiritual battle" (CCC 405), if we persevere in following Christ, grace affords the possibility of "a real and deep victory" in this battle (see TOB 45:4). As the Council of Trent expressed it, concupiscence " 'is left for us to wrestle with.' " However, we are also able to " 'resist it by the grace of Jesus Christ' " (see CCC 1264). In other words, by the grace of Christ, which he never fails to give us if we but ask, we can overcome concupiscent desire. Even more, as John Paul II teaches, in Christ and with Christ we encounter the possibility "*of transforming* what has been weighed down by the concupiscence of the flesh" (TOB 47:5).

As John Paul II insists, Christ's words about overcoming concupiscent desire in the Sermon on the Mount "are not a call hurled into emptiness. They do not address the man who is completely bound by the concupiscence of the flesh." Rather, Christ's words testify to the *real power* of redemption at work in "the very 'nature,' the very substrate of the humanity of the person, the deepest impulses of the 'heart' " (TOB 46:5). This means that following Christ involves much more than taking up a (more or less successful) program of "sin management." The "program" we must take up in following Christ is the arduous, life-long journey towards "a full purification" (TOB 116:3).

As John Paul makes clear, "Christ does not invite man to return to the state of original innocence, because humanity has left it irrevocably behind." Rather, Christ calls us to find "the *living forms of the 'new man.'* In this way a connection is formed, even a continuity, between the 'beginning' and the perspective of redemption. In the ethos of the redemption of the body, the original ethos of creation was to be taken up anew" (TOB 49:4). "The words of Christ testify that *the original power* (and thus also the grace) *of the mystery of creation becomes* for each of [us] *the power* (that is, the grace) *of the mystery of redemption*" (TOB 46:5).

The New Ethos of Redemption

Christ begins his teaching about lust with a reference to the law of Moses: "You have heard that it was said, 'You shall not commit adultery.'" However, Christ's further words, "But I say to you . . . ," show that the law alone was not enough. The Law "does not of itself give the strength, the grace of the Spirit, to fulfill it. Because of sin, which [the Law] cannot remove, it remains a law of bondage" (CCC 1963). Hence, as John Paul II insists, there is something "new" being offered to us in the Sermon on the Mount. That "newness" is precisely "*the possibility and the necessity of transforming* what has been weighed down by the concupiscence of the flesh" (TOB 47:5). Indeed, the "new dimension of ethos is always linked," as John Paul

II maintained, "with the liberation of the heart from 'concupiscence'" (TOB 43:6).

So we can see here not only that John Paul teaches transformation of our concupiscent desires is *possible*; he insists that it is *necessary* if we are to live what he terms "the ethos of redemption," or, "more precisely, the ethos of the redemption of the body" (TOB 49:2). "Ethos," in the language of John Paul, refers to the inner desire and orientation of our hearts—what attracts us and what repulses us: that is our own personal *ethos*. "Ethic," on the other hand, refers to the objective norm or law. Thus, in the Sermon on the Mount, Christ is saying something like this: "You've heard the *ethic* not to commit adultery. But the problem is your *ethos* is off. I'm not here just to reinforce the law. I want to transform your lustful hearts." This is why in the "New" Testament we have "without a doubt *a 'new' ethos*. It is 'new' *in comparison with the ethos of the men of the Old Testament* . . . It is also 'new' in comparison with the state of 'historical' man *after original sin, that is, in comparison with the 'man of concupiscence.'* It is, therefore, a new ethos in . . . relation to every human being" (TOB 49:1).

In effect, if all we've been given when it comes to Church teaching on sex is a list of rules to follow, then we have yet to "pass over" from the Old to the New

Testaments. What's *new* about the New Testament? "The law was given through Moses; grace and truth came through Jesus Christ" (Jn 1:17). It's precisely the fact that we are given "grace upon grace" (Jn 1:16) to transform our hearts, to transform our desires and thus "fulfill the law"—this is what is *new* about the New Testament. As the *Catechism* teaches, in the "Sermon on the Mount . . . the Spirit of the Lord gives new form to our desires, those inner movements that animate our lives" (CCC 2764).

A New Ethos of "Seeing"

To show this "newness" John Paul compares and contrasts Christ's teaching in the Sermon on the Mount with some of the admonitions about lust in the Wisdom literature of the Old Testament. The following passage from *Theology of the Body Explained* provides a good summary of John Paul II's teaching on the matter of "liberation from the domination of concupiscence" as I have come to understand it:

> True to their name, [the Wisdom] books contain great wisdom. They reveal an intimate knowledge of the human heart and even develop a specific moral psychology. In this way, the Wisdom books "are in some way close to Christ's appeal

to the 'heart' reported by Matthew" (TOB 38:5). Even so, John Paul says that . . . the Wisdom texts do not change man's ethos in any fundamental way. "Such a transformation of ethos had to await the Sermon on the Mount" (TOB 38:6). For example, whereas the Wisdom texts offer understandable admonitions such as "Turn away your eyes from a shapely woman" (Sir 9:8), John Paul says that in the Sermon on the Mount Christ invites us "to a pure way of looking at others, capable of respecting the spousal meaning of the body" (VS 15).

As experience attests, the battle with lust remains fierce. For the man bound by lust, "Turn away your eyes" retains all its wisdom. Christ, however, "speaks in the context of human experience and at the same time in the context of the work of salvation." In the new ethos, these "two contexts in some way superimpose themselves on each other and interpenetrate" (TOB 38:2). This means that, although we all *experience* lust, we can also *experience* a real transformation of our hearts through the *salvation* Christ offers us . . .

Christ did not die on a cross and rise from the dead merely to give us coping mechanisms for sin (we already had plenty of those without a savior).[23] Christ died and rose again to set us free from sin. To the degree that a man's heart has been transformed and vivified by the Spirit of the Lord, he need not merely "cope" with lust by turning his eyes away from a woman (or a woman from a man). Through continual death and resurrection, our desires take on "new form." The more we grow in mastery of ourselves, the more we experience a proper "ethos of seeing" (TOB 63:6). We become empowered to look at others purely—and not only to "look" but to see others purely, to see the true beauty of the person revealed, not despite the body, but in and through the body.

This is a "new" ethos in relation to that of the Wisdom texts, which seem to presuppose bondage to concupiscence. In this new ethos, the pope tells us elsewhere,

> we come to an ever greater awareness of the gratuitous beauty of the human body, of masculinity and femininity . . . With the passage of time, if we persevere in following Christ our Teacher, we feel less and less burdened by the struggle against

> sin, and we enjoy more and more the divine light which pervades all creation. This is most important, because it allows us to escape from a situation of constant inner exposure to the risk of sin—even though, on this earth, the risk always remains present to some degree—so as to move with ever greater freedom within the whole created world. This same freedom and simplicity characterizes our relations with other human beings, including those of the opposite sex. (MI, p. 29) (TOBE, pp. 212-214)

The more we experience this "new ethos of seeing," the more we appreciate the divine light reflected in the sacramentality of the human body. As Christ put it: "If your eye is sound, your whole body will be filled with light" (Mt 6:22). The more sound our eyes are, the more we come to see others with eyes of love and as transparent icons of divine love. To the degree that we experience this new way of "seeing," we have "passed over" from the Old Testament ethos to the New Testament ethos, and we are empowered not only to meet the law's demands, but to fulfill the law.

Admittedly, in a world immersed in the mire of a pornographic vision of things, this "new ethos of seeing" can seem not only impossible, but unimaginable. Sometimes it's all we can do just to avoid the pull of lustful temptations and "flee from the fire," so to speak. In light of that fact, this "new ethos of seeing" seems to raise the bar to an impossibly high standard, does it not? If we are looking only at our own weaknesses, yes, it *is* an impossibly high standard. "The Church is aware of these weaknesses," as John Paul II stated. "At the same time," he continued, the Church "cannot renounce her faith in redeemed man, she cannot renounce the conviction that for all man's weakness, he '*can* do all things in him who strengthens' him (Phil 4:13)." The good news is that grace "is more powerful than the weaknesses endemic in the human heart" (BNA, p. 118). Thus, this "new ethos of seeing" is possible not based on man's own ability, but "only as a result of a gift of God who heals, restores, and transforms the human heart by his grace" (VS 23).

At the same time, this inner transformation "demands an intense spiritual commitment and is no stranger to painful purifications (the 'dark night')" (NMI 33). As we persevere through a myriad of struggles, trials, falls, and setbacks, these painful purifications are precisely what lead us more and more to a mature purity of heart.[24] "We cannot acquire this purity without renunciation, without struggles against our own inner weakness," as John Paul II once observed. However, "once acquired, this maturity of heart and mind makes up a hundredfold for the efforts it rewards. The result is a new spontaneity of feeling, of gesture, and of behavior." In turn, we discover "values that are only revealed to the pure vision and the pure heart" (BNA, p. 16).

Attaining this "maturity of heart" and this "pure vision" is a task given to every man and woman (see CCC 2013, 2545; see also VS 18). However, as I wrote in *Theology of the Body Explained,* getting there

> is certainly a fragile journey demanding a lifetime of diligent effort and arduous struggle. Victory does not come overnight, nor can one ever claim to have accomplished a permanent victory in this life (see CCC 2342). Because lust will always be a reality in a fallen world, we will always need God's mercy. But the grace of his mercy enables us to attain a mature level of purity. No matter how deep our wounds and distortions go, the cross of Christ goes deeper, and John Paul continually insists that *real power* flows from Christ's death and resurrection to

> restore in us the purity that was lost through sin. Our struggle with concupiscence will only cease in the eschaton, but as the *Catechism* teaches: "Even now [purity of heart] enables us to see *according to* God." It "lets us perceive the human body—ours and our neighbor's—as a temple of the Holy Spirit, a manifestation of divine beauty" (CCC 2519). (TOBE, p. 214)

An Example of "Mature Purity"

"In mature purity," writes the late Holy Father, "man enjoys the fruits of victory over concupiscence" (TOB 58:7). In order to demonstrate the difference between this "mature" kind of purity, on the one hand, and the beginning stages of purity on the other, I often tell a story about two bishops and their differing reactions to a scantily clad prostitute. Here's how I report this story in my book *Theology of the Body Explained*:

> Two bishops walked out of a cathedral just as a scantily clad prostitute passed by. One bishop immediately turned away. The other bishop looked at her intently. The bishop who turned away exclaimed, "Brother bishop, what are you doing? Turn your eyes!" When the bishop turned

around, he lamented with tears streaming down his face, "How tragic that such beauty is being sold to the lusts of men." Which one of these bishops was *vivified* with the ethos of redemption? Which one had passed over from merely meeting the demands of the law to a super-abounding fulfillment of the law?

As an important clarification, the bishop who turned his eyes *did the right thing,* since he knew that if he had not done so he would have lusted. We classically call this "avoiding the occasion of sin" by "gaining custody of the eyes." This is a commendable and necessary first step on the road to a mature purity. But it is only a first step. We are called to more. The bishop who turned away desired the good with his will, but his need to turn away in order to avoid lusting demonstrates that concupiscence still dominated his heart. As the *Catechism* teaches, the "perfection of the moral good consists in man's being moved to the good not only by his will but also by his 'heart' " (CCC 1775). To the degree that our hearts are transformed through ongoing conversion to Christ, our purity matures, enabling us to see the body for what it is: a sign that makes visible the invisible mystery hidden in God from time

> immemorial. To the degree that we cannot see this, the distortions of sin still blind us.
>
> I am not suggesting the average man should look for opportunities to "test" his purity by gazing upon scantily clad women. Indeed, the large majority of men must heed the Old Testament admonition to "turn away your eyes." But for anyone who doubts that the purity of the "bishop who looked" is possible, I must add that the above example is adapted from the story of Bishop St. Nonnus of Edessa and the harlot Pelagia. Stories of their encounter differ and the details are sketchy. But it is generally reported that upon seeing the half-naked Pelagia parading through the streets of Antioch while his brother bishops turned away, Bishop Nonnus looked upon her with love and great delight. She noticed his look of love and was eventually converted through his counsel and preaching. She is known as St. Pelagia of Antioch. (TOBE, pp. 215-216)[25]

The point of the story is this: mature purity involves more than "looking away." In the Sermon on the Mount, Christ is inviting us on a journey of inner purification that gradually enables us to "see" as he sees. The more we gaze with faith upon Christ, the more "his gaze purifies our heart." In turn, "the light of the countenance of Jesus illumines the eyes of our heart and teaches us to see everything in the light of his truth" (CCC 2715). In this sense, our ability to "see everything in light of Christ's truth" becomes a measure of the conversion of our hearts to Christ, a measure of our degree of "participation" in the risen life of Christ (which means, of course, we all have a long way to go before our hearts are completely converted to Christ).

We will only know the fullness of this "risen life" in the general resurrection at the end of time. However, as the *Catechism* teaches, "Christian life is already now on earth a participation in the death and Resurrection of Christ" (CCC 1002). This means that even now purity of heart can enable us to see the beauty of the human body according to God (see CCC 2519). As St. John Climacus wrote: "Someone, I was told, at the sight of a very beautiful body, felt impelled to glorify the Creator. The sight of it increased his love for God to the point of tears. Anyone who entertains such feelings in such circumstances is already risen . . . before the general resurrection" (*The Ladder of Divine Ascent,* fifteenth step).

Of course, even those with a mature purity can still slip and fall. Growth in virtue is not simply a steady uphill climb. This means no one could ever claim in this life that he or she is entirely beyond the need for "custody of the eyes." Our adversary is always on the prowl like a lion in search of someone to devour (see I Pt 5:8). As I wrote in *Theology of the Body for Beginners*:

> Let me emphasize—if this isn't clear enough already—that the "positive" approach to purity I'm outlining with the Pope's help does not provide a license to "push the envelope." The person who uses anything in this book as an excuse to indulge his (or her) lusts isn't seeking purity. Honest people know their limits. They know what situations would make them stumble and avoid them with the seriousness Christ demands of us. "If your right eye causes you to sin, pluck it out . . . if your right hand causes you to sin, cut it off" (Mt 5:29-30). Modern adaptation: "If your computer causes you to sin, throw it away. If your TV causes you to sin, get rid of it." (TOBB, p. 48)

Continence and Virtue

One of the reasons I tell the story of the two bishops is to illuminate the important distinction that St. Thomas Aquinas makes between "continence" and "virtue." In

Thomas's language, a person who merely resists the impulse to sin demonstrates *continence* in that area, but not true *virtue.*[26] Thomas writes that continence

> falls short of being virtue: since intellectual virtue, which makes reason to hold itself well in respect of moral matters, presupposes a right desire of the end . . . and this is lacking in the continent and persevering man . . . Hence if the sensitive faculty, which is moved by the rational faculty, is not perfect; however perfect the rational faculty may be, the resulting action will be imperfect: and consequently the principle of that action will not be a virtue. And for this reason, continence, desisting from pleasures, and perseverance in the midst of pains, are not virtues, but something less than virtue . . . (*Summa Theologica*, Prima Secundae, q. 58, a. 3, ad 2)

From this perspective, we can see that the bishop who looked away was *continent,* whereas the bishop who experienced the new "ethos of seeing" was *virtuous.* Continence in this sense is an absolutely essential step along the road to mature chastity, and it is commendable to be sure. But this "falls short of being virtue."[27] The point is that "virtue" is more than the successful resistance of one's disordered passions. As the *Catechism* says, human virtues "order our passions . . . They make possible ease, self-mastery, and joy in leading a morally good life" (CCC 1804). In his book *Love and Responsibility,* the future John Paul II made the same distinction when he wrote that the "ability merely to subdue the appetites originating in sensuality as they arise falls short of virtue, it is not chastity in the full sense of the word, even if the individual concerned nearly always succeeds in controlling himself. Fully formed virtue," he continued, "is an efficiently functioning control which permanently keeps the appetites in equilibrium by means of its habitual attitude to the true good" (LR, p. 169).

G. K. Chesterton made the same point: "Virtue is not the absence of vices or the avoidance of moral dangers; virtue is a vivid and separate thing . . . Chastity [therefore] does not mean abstention from sexual wrong; it means something flaming, like Joan of Arc" (*The Daily News,* November 4, 1905). What an image! Chastity means to be set on fire, lit up in flames at the stake of love like Joan of Arc! In other words—contrary to popular wisdom—we overcome lust not by trying to "snuff out the fire." We overcome the fire of lust by entering into an infinitely greater Fire, that of God's Eros-Agape love. As St. John Climacus put it: "The chaste one is he who drives out eros with Eros" (cited in TF 4). Oh Lord, come with your Fire, come set us ablaze!

Growth in Virtue Comes Only Through Renunciation and Sacrifice

But how do we come to experience this kind of virtue? If we are to fight fire with Fire, eros with Eros, then we must also recognize that the journey from the lowercase to the uppercase, shall we say, passes by way of consistent discipline, renunciation, and sacrifice. We must learn, as St. Paul says, how to "crucify our flesh" with its lustful desires (see Gal 5:24). Here are some examples from past writings in which I speak of this life of prayerful discipline and renunciation:[28]

> To grow in purity, the Pope says we must devote ourselves to "a progressive education in self-control of the will, of sentiments, of emotions, which must be developed from the simplest gestures, in which it is relatively easy to put the inner decision into practice" (TOB, 128:1). For example, what are your eating habits? If you can't say no to a potato chip, how are you going to say no to indulging in lust? Fasting is a wonderful way to grow in mastery of our passions. If this isn't already part of your life, start with a simple

sacrifice that's relatively easy to put into practice. As you continue exercising this "muscle," you will find your strength increasing. What was once "impossible" gradually becomes possible.

> . . . Rather than repress lust by pushing it into the subconscious, trying to ignore it, or otherwise seeking to annihilate it, we must *surrender* our lusts to Christ and allow him to slay them. As we do, "the Spirit of the Lord gives new form to our desires" (CCC 2764). In other words, as we allow lust to be "crucified," we also come to experience the "resurrection" of God's original plan for sexual desire. Not immediately, but gradually, progressively, as we take up our cross every day and follow, we come to experience sexual desire as the power to love in God's image . . . To reinforce your decision to "die" to lust, you may also want to place yourself in the shape of a cross—hands outstretched . . . The point here is to conform yourself to Christ, to carry "in the body the death of Jesus, so that the life of Jesus may also be manifested in your bodies" (2 Cor 4:10).

Resolving *not* to indulge lust can be very difficult, at times even emotionally and physically wrenching. It seems few men and women experience

> the freedom for which Christ has set us free because when they taste this kind of "crucifixion," rather than staying the course which leads to resurrection, they "come down from the cross." When those nails are biting into your hands, and the burden of the cross seems too heavy to bear, keep going! You are on the verge of a passover from death to life, from lust to authentic love. Only if we are willing to die with Christ can we also live the resurrected life he offers. (TOBB, pp. 47-48)

The following is a reflection on Pope Benedict XVI statement: "Purification and growth in maturity are called for; and these also pass through the path of renunciation. Far from rejecting or 'poisoning' *eros,* they heal it and restore its true grandeur" (DC 5).

> "Self-mastery is a *long and exacting work.* One can never consider it acquired once and for all. It presupposes renewed effort at all stages of life" (CCC 2342).[29] It demands renunciation of lust, the warped and destructive form of *eros,* but Christian renunciation does not involve the "annihilation" of anything authentically human. Christian renunciation involves a certain kind of "death," but *always* with a view to resurrection.

Lust must die so that *eros* can be resurrected in its true grandeur. *Eros* loses nothing of its essence with the death of lust. Rather, it is liberated from what distorts it so that it might become what it truly is: a human way of expressing divine love.

Without setting our eyes on this restoration or *resurrection* of *eros,* we can only conceive of renunciation as Nietzsche did—as a "poisoning" of *eros,* as a great big "no" that stifles the natural spontaneity of the sexual relationship. But this is a superficial perspective. The discipline required in living *eros* as a virtue (love) rather than as a vice (lust) does not stifle or harm the sexual relationship. Rather, it enlarges it, enriches it, liberates it, sublimates it, and beautifies it.

I once heard the following analogy given to explain the difference between the spontaneity of lust and love. Anyone can "spontaneously" bang on piano keys and make meaningless noise. A concert pianist can also spontaneously tickle the keys and make music that lifts the soul to the heavens. But everyone knows that behind the "spontaneity" of the concert pianist is a lifetime of quiet discipline, sacrifice, and renunciation. The spontaneity of an undisciplined *eros* can

> only lead to meaningless noise. The Christian view of *eros,* when properly understood and lived, instills the discipline that allows men and women to make spontaneous music that lifts them to the heavens . . . But, again, such beautiful music comes only at the price of countless acts of sacrifice. (LS, pp. 37-39)

The call to make this kind of "beautiful music" is precisely the call to the mature virtue of chastity in which, through much discipline, we learn "step by step," as John Paul says (see TOB 45:3) how to direct our desires and affections towards that which is true, good, and beautiful. This does not necessarily mean a steady uphill climb. There can be just as many great slips as there are great strides, and just as many small failings as there are small gains. But, with God's grace, we can progress towards a mature level of virtue. And this is not just intended for a select few. As the *Catechism* maintains: "All Christ's faithful are to 'direct their affections rightly'" (CCC 2545).

Suspicion and Determinism in the Sexual Sphere

Some Christians seem to believe that such virtue lies beyond man's concrete possibilities. From one perspective, they're correct. For, as Wojtyla observed: "*Man, alas, is not such a perfect being that the sight of the body of another person, especially a person of the other sex, can arouse in him merely a disinterested liking which develops into an innocent affection.* In practice, it also arouses concupiscence, or a wish to enjoy concentrated on sexual values with no regard for the value of the person" (LR, p. 190). This, indeed, is the common experience of fallen man. But man is not merely fallen; he is also *redeemed* (see TOB 45:3).[30] In this context John Paul asks: "[W]hat are the 'concrete possibilities of man'? And of which man are we speaking? Of man *dominated* by lust or of man *redeemed by Christ.* This is what is at stake: the *reality* of Christ's redemption. *Christ has redeemed us!* This means he has given us the possibility of realizing the *entire truth* of our being; he has set our freedom free from the *domination* of concupiscence" (VS 103).

It's all too easy to "measure the divine power according to [our] own narrow minds." Indeed, as St. Thérèse of Lisieux observed, "those souls are rare who don't" (SOS, p. 209). *"Ne evacuetur Crux!"*—John Paul II exclaims, "Do not empty the Cross of its power!" (see 1 Cor 1:17). "This," he said, "is the cry of the new evangelization." For "if the cross of Christ is emptied of its power, man no longer has roots, he no longer has prospects: he is destroyed" (OL 3). Indeed, if the cross of Christ is emptied of its power, we fall prey to what John Paul II calls "the hermeneutic [or interpretation] of suspicion"—an attitude that, in the end, does not fully believe that mature virtue is possible in the sexual realm (see TOB 46).

It's been said, for example, in reference to the story of the two bishops, that the only way a man could look at a prostitute without sinning is if he were "insensitive" to sex. John Paul II is very critical of this kind of "determinism in the sexual sphere," as he called it in a pre-papal essay. Such determinism tends "to limit the possibility of virtue and magnify the 'necessity of sin' in this sphere." John Paul II's approach, however, entails "the opposite tendency," as he himself wrote. It upholds "the possibility of virtue, based on self-control and sublimation [which means to raise up, make sublime]" (PC, p. 286). As John Paul insists: "*Man cannot stop at casting the 'heart' into a state of* continual and irreversible *suspicion* due to the manifestations of the concupiscence of the flesh . . . Redemption is a truth, a reality, in the name of which man must feel himself called, and 'called with effectiveness'" (TOB 46:4).

Does the effectiveness of this redemption grant one only the ability to "gain custody of the eyes"? Or can the grace of redemption allow us gradually to progress beyond that preliminary stage in order to reclaim something of the original good of the divine vision? The teaching of John Paul II is clear: "With the passage of time, if we persevere in following Christ our Teacher, we feel less and less burdened by the struggle against sin" (MI, p. 29) and we come to discover "a pure way of looking at others, capable of respecting the spousal meaning of the body" (VS 15).

"Custody of the eyes may sometimes be a sensible prudential tactic," writes Father Simon Tugwell, "but it is a doubtful philosophy of life. We shall not see God the more clearly for narrowing our vision. Purity of heart clarifies vision . . . Where cynicism sees through all that is beautiful and good and simple, to find murkiness within, purity of heart sees through ugliness and sin and pain and failure to find God within" (BSCT, p. 103). "Blessed are the pure of heart, for they shall see God."

Oh, God, take us into your fire, transform our desire; grant us purity of heart! St. Joan of Arc, pray for us!

Chapter 5

The Great Analogy of Spousal Love

The Prophets describe God's passion for his people using boldly erotic images.

—Pope Benedict XVI (DC 9)

The central proclamation of John Paul II's TOB is that the body, precisely in the "great mystery" of its creation as male and female and the call of the two to become "one flesh," was created by God to be the primordial sign of his own "Great Mystery": his eternal exchange of Love and our destiny to share in that exchange through the holy nuptials of Christ's union with the Church. The tragedy of sin, however, is that—subjectively speaking—the body "loses its character as a sign" (TOB 40:4). Blinded by sin, we no longer see and experience the body as the primordial revelation of the divine plan of love. Rather, we see and experience the body primarily as an object that arouses concupiscence.

Can we recognize the diabolic coup at work here? Think for a moment with the mind of the Enemy. If the purpose of our creation as male and female and the call of the two to become "one flesh" is to point us to heaven, and if there's an enemy who wants to keep us from heaven, where is he going to aim his most potent arrows? The devil is not creative. He cannot produce his own "evil world" apart from God's "very good" world. All he can do is take the good things God created and twist them, distort them, or mock them. And, of course, he sets his sights on the primordial sign of the divine mystery. By mocking the body and the one-flesh union, he twists their "theo-graphic" nature into something "porno-graphic."

It is sobering to realize that the diabolic plot behind the pornographic culture in which we live has one final aim: to blind us to the "great mystery" revealed through our bodies and thereby foil our participation in the Marriage of the Lamb. It can happen that we become so conditioned by these pornographic lies that they become the default "light" in which we see the body. But when the "light" in which we see the body is actually darkness, the body loses its character as a sign of the "great mystery" and we tend to associate it almost exclusively with what is profane and offensive. We may assent intellectually to the goodness and holiness of the body, but in practice we can't see it because our eyes are not sound. As Jesus said, if our eyes are sound, the entirety of our bodies will be filled with light; but if our eyes are not sound, our bodies will be shrouded in darkness (see Mt 6:22-23).

Reclaiming the Body as a Sign

The following analogy might help illuminate the above point. A friend of mine who counsels those coming out of satanic cults has shared with me the particular difficulties involved in their healing. In a "black mass" there is a mock "liturgy of the word," mock "prayers of the faithful" (curses are invoked), and a mock "liturgy of the Eucharist" in which a satanic priest offers a mock-sacrifice on a candlelit altar.

One can imagine two scenarios when those who have been repeatedly conditioned by these sacrileges encounter the true Mass. Through a divine gift of illumination, a person might "see" the devil's coup immediately, come out of the darkness, and enter the divine light that pervades the rituals of the true liturgy. Or, because of how "dark the darkness" has been, a person might be re-traumatized at a Catholic Mass by what the altar and the candles and the priest evoke. The latter, according to my friend, is common. Some of his counselees, he says, even though they love the Lord and strive to live their faith, find it too difficult even to enter a Catholic church. One must be very patient, loving, and understanding with such people as they learn to untwist the diabolic distortions and reclaim the true meaning of liturgical symbols. Only slowly, and with much difficulty, are they able to experience their real meaning and saving power.

The Church—in Sacred Scripture, in the teaching of her saints, and even in her liturgical rituals—makes use of some "boldly erotic images" to help us enter in to the "great mystery" of Christ's love for us. This sacred spousal imagery flows from the very logic of the theology of our bodies. However, just as those exposed to the mockeries of a "black mass" can find it very difficult to enter a church, it can be very difficult to enter the "theo-graphic" meaning of the body when we've been wounded by the mockeries of a porno-graphic culture. Furthermore, just as those counseling people coming out of the "black mass" must be very patient and gentle in introducing them to the symbols of the true Mass, so must teachers of the faith be very patient and gentle as they introduce people to the true meaning of the body and the mystical treasures of spousal imagery.[31]

In this chapter, we will unfold why applying sexual imagery (integrally understood) to the mystery of Christ and the Church is not a matter of "degrading" spiritual and supernatural realities by "sexualizing" them, as some assert. Rather, as John Paul II wrote, it is a matter of explaining "spiritual and supernatural [realities] through the likeness of the body and of the love by which the spouses, husband and wife, become 'one flesh'" (TOB 92:3). Here John Paul II's reflections on Ephesians 5 are key.

This Is a "Great Mystery"

It's hard to overstate how important Ephesians 5 is to John Paul II (and to the entire mystical tradition of the Church). Indeed, he sees the teaching of Ephesians 5 on the spousal mystery as "the 'crowning' of the themes" of Sacred Scripture (TOB 87:3). Thus, we must try, he says, to "understand if possible 'to the very depths' what wealth of truth revealed by God is contained within the scope of that stupendous page." Then, referring to his "anthem" from Vatican II, he states that the spousal imagery of Ephesians 5 "'reveals—in a particular way—*man to man himself* and makes *his supreme vocation* clear' (GS 22)" (TOB 87:6).

While St. Paul unfolds various themes in Ephesians 5, we find "the most important point of the whole text, *in some sense its keystone*" (TOB 93:1) in verses 31:32—" 'For this reason a man shall leave his father and mother and be joined to his wife, and the two shall become one flesh.' This is a great mystery, and I mean in reference to Christ and the church." As John Paul II tells us, the one-flesh union of spouses and the mystical union of Christ and the Church are so intimately related that St. Paul brings them together "making of them *the single great sign*, that is, *a great sacrament* ('*sacramentum magnum*')." And it is "a particular merit to the author of Ephesians" that he unites these mysteries in this way (TOB 95b:7).

The "great mystery" revealed in the linking of the one-flesh union with the union of Christ and the Church "*signifies the mystery* first hidden in God's mind and later revealed in man's history. Given its importance, the mystery is *'great' indeed*," John Paul tells us. It reveals "God's salvific plan for humanity," and, as such, "that mystery is in some sense the central theme of the whole of revelation, its central reality. It is what God as Creator and Father wishes above all to transmit to mankind in his Word" (TOB 93:2). In this way, as we learned in Chapter 1, "Saint Paul's magnificent synthesis concerning the 'great mystery' appears as the compendium or *summa,* in some sense, *of the teaching about God and man* which was brought to fulfillment by Christ" (LF 19).

These are incredibly provocative statements, warranting deep, prayerful reflection. John Paul II posits the idea that what God wishes "above all" to tell the human race about his "salvific plan for humanity" is summarized in Ephesians 5, and, more specifically, in verses 31-32. Here—in the "great mystery" of the intimate link between sexual love[32] and Christ's love for the Church—we find a kind of compendium of Christ's teaching about who God is, who we are, and the relationship God wants to have with us. Stunning! No wonder we all have a longing to understand the meaning of our bodies: we're looking for the divine mystery.

Christianity "Clothes" Itself in the Mystery of Marriage

Drawing in a particular way from the mystical teaching of St. John of the Cross,[33] John Paul II uses the spousal mystery—that is, the mystery of masculinity and femininity and the call to spousal love and union—as a "lens" through which to view the entirety of God's plan for man and for the universe as revealed from Genesis to Revelation. As we learn through "*the single great sign*" in Ephesians 5, what is at stake in our view of the human body is not just a proper understanding of the human person, sexuality, and marriage. What is at stake is also a proper understanding of Christ and the Church. What is at stake is the "great mystery" that lies at the heart of the Gospel. This broad and grand scope of the TOB is often missed, even among some scholars who study the works of John Paul II.[34]

The two realms—the bodily/sexual/marital realm and the Christian realm—are so intimately united that they stand or fall together in the mind and heart of man. As our sex understanding goes—and by this I mean our understanding of our incarnate creation as male and female and the call of the two to become "one flesh" in the sacrament of marriage—so goes our understanding of Christ and the Church. Reflecting on this link between spousal union and the mystical union of Christ and the Church, John Paul II states:

> The Church cannot therefore be understood as the mystical body of Christ, as the sign of man's covenant with God in Christ, or as the universal sacrament of salvation, unless we keep in mind the 'great mystery' involved in the creation of man as male and female and the vocation of both to

> conjugal love, to fatherhood and to motherhood. The "great mystery," which is the Church and humanity in Christ, does not exist apart from the "great mystery" expressed in the "one flesh," that is, in the reality of marriage and the family. (LF 19)

Why can't we understand the "great mystery" of the Church and humanity in Christ apart from the union of spouses in "one flesh"? Because the mystery of our redemption in Christ "clothes itself," John Paul tells us "in the figure and form of the primordial sacrament" (TOB 97:2). Marriage is that "primordial sacrament"—the fundamental, first, and original revelation of the divine Mystery inscribed in the very order of creation. This means, moreover, that right from the beginning, marriage was an "efficacious sign"—that is, it really communicated the divine life to man and woman (see TOB 19:4). And it did so, John Paul maintains, in light of Christ "while chronologically anticipating his coming in the body" (TOB 96:5). For God chose us in Christ *not only after we sinned* and in order to redeem us from sin. God chose us in Christ "before the foundation of the world" (Eph 1:4). And all this was realized in and through the "primordial sacrament."[35]

While marriage lost its ability to communicate the divine life as a result of sin (see TOB 97:1), it was "resurrected" in this ability through the mystery of redemption (see TOB 100:2). And here, in the mystery of redemption, marriage is not just one of the seven sacraments. Marriage "has arisen from redemption *in the form . . . of a 'prototype'* . . . If we reflect deeply on this dimension, we have to conclude that all the sacraments of the New Covenant find their prototype in some way in marriage as the primordial sacrament" (TOB 98:2). For the goal of all of the sacraments—indeed, the goal of the Christian life itself—is to unite us with Christ our Bridegroom in an eternally fruitful union of love. Perhaps we could look at it this way. It's almost as if marriage, the "one and only sacrament" in the mystery of creation (TOB 98:3), was fractured by sin into seven sacraments—like light which, when fractured, reveals seven colors. And just as each color of the rainbow carries forth an aspect of the light from which it derived, analogously each of the seven sacraments bears something of the spousal mystery of the primordial sacrament (see TOBE, p. 433).

Foundation of the Whole Sacramental Order

Now one of John Paul II's most important insights comes to light—an insight which in some way captures the full weight of glory that he believes God has ascribed to marriage and to the union of spouses in "one flesh." It's one of those statements that theologians, no doubt, will chew on for centuries, only gradually unpacking its vast implications: "One can say," John Paul asserts, "that the visible sign of marriage 'in the beginning,' inasmuch as it is linked to the visible sign of Christ and of the Church on the summit of God's saving economy, *transposes* the eternal plan of love *into the 'historical' dimension* and makes it *the foundation of the whole sacramental order*" (TOB 95b:7). Here's how I explain this dense idea in my commentary on TOB:

> If the union of Christ and the Church is "on the summit of God's saving economy," we might say that at the trailhead marking the path to this summit, we have marriage and its consummate expression of conjugal intercourse. Inasmuch as this "trailhead" points to the summit, the visible sign of marriage[36] is the foundation upon which God reveals and actuates his hidden designs—

revealing his plan for man and for the universe that all things in heaven and on earth might be "one" in fruitful union with Jesus Christ (see Eph 1:10). This is the deepest essence and meaning of human embodiment, of erotic desire, and of spousal love. They are meant to point us to Christ and to God's hidden designs for the universe. Thus, inasmuch as the spousal union points us (analogically) to Christ's union with the Church, the visible sign of marriage constitutes "*the foundation of the whole sacramental order*"—that order by which God *incarnates* his own mystery, making it visible in the order of "signs" in order to communicate it to incarnate men and women.

Perhaps now we can sense with what awe and reverence St. Paul referred to the "one flesh" union as "a great mystery." Perhaps now we can better understand what St. Paul means when he calls spouses to submit to one another *out of reverence* for Christ. Words fail when we come in contact with such a mystery. It seems the only proper response is silence offered as praise and tears offered in reparation for the desecration of this sacramental mystery so prevalent in our world and often in our own hearts. (TOBE, p. 417)

Summit of the Sacramental Order

The "summit of God's saving economy" to which marriage points is, of course, the Eucharist. "The Eucharist is 'the source and summit of the Christian life'" (CCC 1324). And right from the beginning, the holy communion of man and woman consummated when the two become "one flesh" foreshadows the Holy Communion of Christ and the Church consummated when the two become "one body, one spirit" in the Eucharist. As Benedict XVI wrote in his pre-papal work on the liturgy, "In the Eucharist a communion takes place that corresponds to the union of man and woman in marriage. Just as they become 'one flesh,' so in Communion, we all become 'one spirit,' one person, with Christ. The spousal mystery, announced in the Old Testament, of the intimate union of God and man takes place in the Sacrament of the Body and Blood of Christ, precisely through his Passion and in a very real way (see Eph 5:29-32; I Cor 6:17; Gal 3:28)" (SL, p. 142).

The following teaching from Blessed John Paul II on the inherent link between the Holy Communion of the Eucharist and the holy communion of spouses is particularly enlightening:

> Christ is the Bridegroom because "he has given himself": his body has been "given," his blood has been "poured out" (see Lk 22:19-20). In this way "he loved them to the end" (Jn 13:1). The "sincere gift" contained in the Sacrifice of the Cross gives definitive prominence to the spousal meaning of God's love. As the Redeemer of the world, Christ is the Bridegroom of the Church. *The Eucharist is the Sacrament of our Redemption.* It is *the Sacrament of the Bridegroom and of the Bride* . . . Christ is united with his "body" as the bridegroom with the bride. All this is contained in the Letter to the Ephesians. The perennial "unity of the two" that exists between man and woman from the very "beginning" is introduced into this "great mystery" of Christ and the Church. (MD 26)

John Paul II goes so far as to say that since Christ linked the Eucharist so closely to the masculinity of the first Apostles (the first priests), through the Eucharist, Christ "wished to express the relationship between man and woman, between what is 'feminine' and what is 'masculine.' It is a relationship willed by God in both the mystery of creation and in the mystery of Redemption" (MD 26). I reflect on this as follows in my TOB commentary:

> The deepest truth of human sexuality, according to John Paul II, is revealed through the Eucharist. In fact, in giving us *his body* in the Eucharist—the gift of *himself* as Bridegroom—Christ wanted to reveal the deepest meaning of *our bodies* as male and female. It is in the Eucharist that Christ fully reveals man to himself and makes his supreme calling clear! Conversely, when all the confusion is cast out and all the distortions untwisted, we discover that the deepest meaning of human sexuality is its signification of the Eucharist. The holy communion of man and woman in "one flesh" is a great mystery that is meant to signify the Holy Communion of Christ and the Church consummated in the Eucharist. (TOBE, p. 25)

Two Directions of the Spousal Analogy

From all that has been said, we can see that the analogy in Ephesians 5 between the holy communion of spouses (consummated when the two become "one flesh") and the Holy Communion of Christ and the Church (consummated in the Eucharist) works in two directions, as John Paul tells us (see TOB 90:4). Spousal love and the love of Christ and the Church are two "great signs" which mutually illuminate each other. Spousal love illuminates both the "unitive" and "life-giving" dimensions of Christ's love for the Church (see TOB 97:4), while Christ's love for the Church illuminates the theological and redemptive dimensions of spousal love (see TOB 102:4). These, among other things, are conclusions John Paul draws from the profound "oneness" of these two great signs. Recall his statement: "It is a particular merit of the author of Ephesians that he brought these two signs together [the sign of the union of spouses in one-flesh, and the sign of the union of Christ and the Church], making of them *the single great sign*, that is, *a great sacrament* (*'sacramentum magnum'*)" (TOB 95b:7).

In exploring the "oneness" of these two great signs, it is critically important, of course, that we do not "sexualize God"—for that is to make him something that he is not: "God is pure spirit in which there is no place for the difference between the sexes" (CCC 370). That said, in light of the Incarnation, it is equally critical that we do not "de-sexualize" Christ—for that is to make him something that he is not: a neutered, disincarnate phantom. The second person of the Trinity took on flesh—*male* flesh born of *female* flesh. From this perspective, one cannot "sexual-ize" Christ;[37] that is, one cannot *make* Christ sexual. He already *is* sexual, that is, he is incarnate as a *male*. To say Christ is sexual does *not* mean he is full of lustful desire as we tend to be in our sexuality. But he did love his Bride with a human love, and that love "may certainly be called *eros*," according to Pope Benedict XVI (DC 9). Nor, when we say Christ is sexual, does it mean that he engaged in genital acts. Once again, to say Christ is sexual is to recognize that he is incarnate as a *male*. And Christ's maleness, his sexuality, is of utmost importance to a proper understanding of Christianity, as is Mary's femaleness.

Virginal Does Not Mean Asexual

Precisely because we tend to believe that lust is the only prism through which to view sexuality, the temptation to "de-sexualize" Christ (and Christianity) is constant and fierce. For it is much easier to "de-sexualize" Christ than it is to "de-lust" our view of sexuality. And it *must* be one or the other, for we instinctively recognize the incompatibility of Christ and lust. But it is Christ and *lust* that are incompatible; *not* Christ and sexuality. Hence, there must be some prism other than lust through which to understand and live one's sexuality. It is precisely this other "prism" that John Paul II presents to us in his TOB. And that prism is Christ and his body "given up for us"—his *male* body, his *Bridegroom* body given for his *Bride.*

There is a widespread tendency to dis-incarnate and neuter our faith, to *un*-flesh our *en*-fleshed Lord. This kind of "neutering" is clear evidence of a failure to see any theological significance in the fact that it is a *male* (Christ, the New Adam, the Bridegroom) who hangs on the cross and a *female* (Mary, the New Eve, symbol of the Church, the Bride) who receives his redemptive gift at the foot of the cross. "The cross gives birth to a new fruitfulness," Angelo Cardinal Scola tells us. And this fruitfulness, while certainly virginal "is by no means asexual" (NM, p. 270). The fruitfulness of the cross is obviously not the result of genital union. But it *is* the result of a mystical union of hearts between a *male* and a *female* and is thus "by no means asexual." In other words, the fruitfulness of the cross is in no way displaced or cut off from the sexuality (the maleness) of the Bridegroom-Christ who hangs on the cross and the sexuality (the femaleness) of the Bride-Church—symbolized here by Mary—at the foot of the cross.

"Mary goes before us all in the holiness that is the Church's mystery as 'the bride without spot or wrinkle,'" says the *Catechism of the Catholic Church* (CCC 773; see also

1138). *The Baltimore Catechism* put it this way: "In the flesh Mary was his Mother, but in the spirit she was his bride" (lesson 35). "The first clue," says Pope Benedict (for this vision of the relationship of Jesus and Mary at the cross) "comes from [Christ's] form of address to Mary: 'Woman.' Jesus had used this same form of address at the marriage feast of Cana (Jn 2:4). The two scenes are thus linked together. Cana had been an anticipation of the definitive marriage feast—of the new wine that the Lord wanted to bestow." The pope elaborates: "The name 'Woman' points back in the first instance to the account of creation, when the Creator presents the woman to Adam [who says] ' . . . she shall be called Woman . . . ' (Gen 2:23)." Jesus, of course, is "the new Adam," and, here, at the foot of the cross, John's Gospel "shows us 'the Woman' who belongs now to this new Adam" (JN2, p. 221). We can enter even more deeply into the evolution of this idea, Pope Benedict tells us,

> in the Letter to the Ephesians, where the saying about the man who leaves his father and mother to become one flesh with his wife is applied to Christ and the Church (see 5:31-32). On the basis of the "corporate personality" model—in keeping with biblical thought—the early Church

> had no difficulty recognizing in the Woman, on the one hand, Mary herself and, on the other hand, transcending time, [recognizing] the Church, bride and mother, in which the mystery of Mary spreads out into history. (JN2, p. 222)

Precisely by receiving the spousal gift of the "new Adam" at the foot of the cross, this "Woman" becomes the virgin mother of all "beloved disciples" in the order of grace. St. John, therefore, becomes a potent symbol of the fertility of the marriage consummated virginally at the cross. "Woman, behold your son!" And to John he said, "Behold, your mother!" (Jn 19:26-27). Archbishop Fulton Sheen explained this "great mystery" as follows:

> Now we've always thought, and rightly so, of Christ the Son on the cross and the mother beneath him. But that's not the complete picture. That's not the deep understanding. Who is our Lord on the cross? He's the new Adam. Where's the new Eve? At the foot of the cross . . . If Eve became the mother of the living in the natural order, is not this woman at the foot of the cross to become another mother? And so the bridegroom looks down at the bride. He looks at his beloved. Christ looks at his Church. There is here the birth of the Church. As St. Augustine puts

> it, and here I am quoting him verbatim, "The heavenly bridegroom left the heavenly chambers, with the presage of the nuptials before him. He came to the marriage bed of the cross, a bed not of pleasure, but of pain, united himself with the woman, and consummated the union forever. As it were, the blood and water that came from the side of Christ was the spiritual seminal fluid." And so from these nuptials "Woman, there's your son" this is the beginning of the Church. (FS, p. 60)

Some people find themselves very uncomfortable with the idea of applying such intimate spousal imagery to Mary, as if it were an affront somehow to her sacred virginity.[38] But this typically stems from a misunderstanding of the nature of "analogy" and/or from a reluctance to affirm the way that grace builds on nature within the analogy. Let's look at both points.

The Nature of "Analogy"

John Paul II observes: "Analogy—as is well known—indicates at one and the same time similarity and also the lack of identity (that is, substantial dissimilarity)" (TOB 33:3). Any sense in which "sexual imagery" would be interpreted as an affront to Mary's or Jesus's (or the

Church's) virginity simply takes the analogy too far and fails to see the *substantial dissimilarity* between supernatural union/fruitfulness and natural union/fruitfulness.[39] That said, there *is* a certain similarity, and it is that similarity that allows Fulton Sheen and St. Augustine, for example, to speak of "the marriage bed of the cross" and Christ's "spiritual seminal fluid."

In my book *Theology of the Body Explained*, under the heading "Understanding the Spousal Analogy Correctly," I explain these important points as follows:

> In his fine and scholarly work *The Nuptial Mystery*, Angelo Cardinal Scola justly warns of two imbalances to be aware of in understanding the spousal analogy. One involves excess and the other deficiency. An excessive or "maximalist" interpretation, Scola writes, "ultimately tends toward an anthropomorphic deformation of our understanding of God, and even into introducing sexuality into God himself . . . Its underlying logic, whether its proponents intend it to or not, ultimately makes the claim that spousal categories are . . . the only categories fit to illuminate Christian dogma. To move in this direction is to engage in bad theology" (NM, p. 394). For all the value of the spousal analogy, it

is critical (lest we end in heresy!) to recognize its limits . . . It should be obvious that the spousal analogy "cannot offer an adequate and complete understanding of that absolutely transcendent Reality." The divine mystery "remains *transcendent with respect to this analogy* as with respect to any other analogy with which we try to express it in human language" (TOB 95b:1).

Perhaps in response to the "maximalist" imbalance, there are those who run the opposite risk of a "minimalist" interpretation. Scola observes that such thinkers "fight every attempt to give the nuptial mystery theological weight." For them, "spousal vocabulary could at most be likened to the language of the parables (and thus would not have even a symbolic value): nuptial images would be on par with many other biblical images, for example those of the shepherd and his sheep" (NM, p. 395). In response, one must certainly acknowledge that the spousal analogy, like all analogies, is woefully inadequate in its representation of the divine mystery. Yet, if all analogies are inadequate, the biblical evidence and the weight of the theological tradition indicate that the spousal analogy is the *least* inadequate. "In this entire world," John Paul says, "there

> is not a more perfect, more complete image of God, Unity and Community. There is no other human reality which corresponds more, humanly speaking, to that divine mystery" (Homily on the Feast of the Holy Family, December 30, 1988). (TOBE, pp. 28-29)

Grace Builds on Nature

The holy nuptials of the New Adam and the New Eve are virginal, spiritual, mystical. They happen in the order of grace. But grace builds on nature; it does not delete nature or cancel it out. Rather, the order of grace draws from nature. Or, working from the other direction—the order of nature foreshadows and prepares us for the order of grace. It's precisely this truth that makes the spousal analogy "a profoundly real analogy" (SL, p. 141) and gives it theological "gravitas." The analogy in Ephesians 5 "is not only a comparison in the sense of a metaphor," John Paul tells us (TOB 98:8). Instead, "one must admit that the very essence of marriage contains *a particle of the [divine] mystery*. Otherwise, this whole analogy would hang in a void." It "would be deprived of a real basis, as if it had no ground under its feet" (TOB 90:3).

And so it is the natural, bodily reality of marital consummation that serves as the foundation, the model, the "prototype" in some way of the spiritual consummation that takes place on "the marriage bed of the cross." We see another example of grace building on nature in this way in the holy mystery of the virginal conception of Christ. By nature of the real weight of the spousal analogy, there is a two-way illumination taking place here. As John Saward reflects, "The radiance of the virginal conception sheds its beams on every human conception" (RW, p. 13). Conversely, since grace builds on nature, natural conception (in the purity God intends for it) offers a basis, a pattern for understanding *something* of the supernatural fecundity of Christ's conception in the virginal womb of Mary.

Caryll Houselander writes: "Just as no one can have an ordinary child of flesh and blood without there being a union of flesh and blood first, no one can generate spiritual life without first having union with the Spirit. Marriage . . . is only a faint shadow, a kind of symbol, of the wedding of the Spirit of God to humanity; and it is from that wedding that Christ is born into the world [both in Mary and, analogously, in us]. Now the union with the

Holy Spirit . . . sows us with wonderful seed" (RG, p. 84). And St. Bonaventure writes that the Christian "conceives [Christ] mystically by the gift of grace. What is happening here?" Bonaventure asks. "It is nothing other than the heavenly Father by a divine seed, as it were, impregnating the soul and making it fruitful. The power of the Most High comes upon the soul and overshadows it (Lk 1:35)" (*Bringing Forth Christ: Five Feasts of the Child Jesus*).

When she was told that she'd be the mother of the Father's eternal Son, Mary inquired of the angel: "'How can this be, since I have no relations with a man?' And the angel said to her in reply, 'The Holy Spirit will come upon you and the power of the Most High will overshadow you'" (Lk 1:34-35). Here is the precise "passage" from the order of nature to the order of grace; from natural fecundity to supernatural. It is a passage that in no way "negates" nature (that would be Manichaean), but, building on it, and "clothing itself" in its form and figure, takes us into an entirely new, virginal dimension of spousal union and fecundity. For Mary's womb was made fruitful not by physical nuptials and male seed, but by mystical nuptials and the power of the Holy Spirit who, according to the analogy, represents the invisible, immortal "seed" of God the Father.

"The Father, who begot the Son in eternity, also begets him in time as a man," writes John Paul II (address July 31, 1996). He also observes that Mary's virginity is motivated by her "desire for total union with God." "She wanted to be his faithful bride" (address August 7, 1996). As the *Catechism* teaches, "The spousal character of the human vocation in relation to God is fulfilled perfectly in Mary's virginal motherhood" (CCC 505).[40]

In summary, mystical nuptials and supernatural fecundity—such as at the Annunciation and at the Cross—are *analogous* (this is the key word for a proper understanding) to the physical nuptials and natural fecundity of the marital embrace. For—always respecting the "discontinuity"—there is a certain "continuity," John Paul tells us, between the "one flesh" union in the order of creation and the union of Christ and the Church in the order of redemption (see TOB 97:2). Here, in both orders (nature and grace; creation and redemption) it is maleness and femaleness and the call of the two to spousal union (one in a genital sense, the other in a mystical, virginal sense) that serves as a "great sign" that communicates the eternal, divine Mystery. John Paul II expresses all of this theological richness as follows:

> In Ephesians 5:31, when the author appeals to the words of the institution of marriage in Genesis 2:24 ("For this reason a man will leave his father and his mother and unite with his wife, and the two will be one flesh"), and immediately after this declares, "This mystery is great; I say this with reference to Christ and the Church" (Eph 5:32), he seems to point out not only the identity of the Mystery hidden in God from eternity, but also the continuity of its realization between the primordial sacrament . . . [and the sacrament of our redemption]—which was brought about when "Christ loved the Church" . . . in the image of the spousal relation that unites husband and wife in marriage . . . In this way the Mystery hidden from all eternity in God—a mystery that in the beginning in the sacrament of creation became *a visible reality through the union* of the first man and woman in the perspective of marriage—becomes in the sacrament of redemption *a visible reality in the indissoluble union of Christ with the Church,* which the author of Ephesians presents as the spousal union of the two, husband and wife. (TOB 97:2, 4)

Again we must emphasize: all of these spiritual and divine truths are revealed *in and through the body.* This is the logic of the Incarnation. In Christ "the whole fullness of deity dwells bodily" (Col 2:9). Christ's body reveals, proclaims, and communicates the divine mystery. It follows, therefore, that our bodies are "absolutely necessary for the explaining, understanding, and grasping of Christianity."[41] If this is true, it means that between here and the beatific vision, all our discomforts and fears surrounding the body and its various functions must be brought into the healing light radiating from the glorified bodies of the New Adam and the New Eve. And all attempts to evade this need by dis-incarnating Christ and "spiritualizing" our faith must be firmly resisted. Ultimately, whether we realize it or not, such "spiritualizing" is the work of the Enemy, the one who denies Christ come in the flesh (see 1 Jn 4:2-3). The key, again, is to hold the physical and spiritual in their proper balance.[42]

Searching for Balance

Let us again look to the Song of Songs in search of the right balance between the physical and the spiritual. As with all of Scripture, we must hold the human and the divine elements of the Song of Songs together in a potent fruitfulness. For the content of the Song is at one and the same time sexual *and* sacred, physical *and* spiritual.

As John Paul observes, drawing from the work of D. Lys, if we ignore the sacred, the Song appears merely as a secular erotic poem. But if we ignore the sexual, we see the Song merely as an allegory of "spiritual" love and fall into *allegorism.* "It is only by putting these two aspects together that one can read the book in the right way" (see TOB 108: note 97). *That's* the essential (and essentially) Catholic "both-and."

Pope St. Gregory the Great expressed it this way: "Hence it is that in the Song of Songs . . . words are set down that pertain to bodily love, so that the soul, wakened anew out of its listless state by language to which it is accustomed, may heat up and may by the language of a lesser love be aroused to a higher" (see TSS, p. 8). The point, again, is this: we don't skip the "lower" to get to the "higher"; we mustn't deny the sexual to get to the spiritual. We go via the "lower" to get to the "higher"; we make use of holy expressions of physical, sexual love to convey the spiritual and the divine. This mystical use of sexual imagery has biblical roots, of course, that go the whole way back to the Prophets of the Old Testament. As Pope Benedict XVI reminds us, "The Prophets, particularly Hosea and Ezekiel, describe God's passion for his people using boldly erotic images" (DC 9). So do the saints. Father Thomas Loya offers the following list of examples:

> St. John Chrysostom told married couples to remember that Christ united himself to the Church "in a spiritual intercourse."[43] Teresa of Avila writes of ecstasies she experienced in "nuptial union" with Christ.[44] St. Bernard of Clairvaux had mystical experiences of nursing at Mary's breasts.[45] St. Louis de Montfort repeatedly refers to Mary's milk and breasts as a source of consolation for Christians.[46] Bishop Fulton Sheen—assuring his audience that he was quoting St. Augustine verbatim—proclaimed that Christ "came to the marriage bed of the Cross, . . . united himself with the woman [the Church], and consummated the union forever." And he didn't hesitate to share publicly Augustine's idea that the blood and water from Christ's side was, as it were, his "spiritual seminal fluid."[47] For those with eyes to see, these precious theological jewels are not a cause for scandal. They make perfect mystical sense; they are beautiful and profoundly healing. ("Theology of the Body and the New Evangelization," 4marks.com/articles).

We can see in expressions like "spiritual intercourse," "spiritual seminal fluid," and "spiritual milk" the linking of two worlds—the invisible-spiritual-mystical world with the visible-physical-sexual world. This link is based on the very logic of the Incarnation, Christ's descent into the flesh—a descent that "is intended to draw us into a movement of ascent," as the future Pope Benedict said. "God seeks us where we are, not so we can stay there, but so that we can come to be where he is" (SL, p. 123). Hence, employing physical, sexual imagery to describe the mysteries of our faith is *not* a matter of reducing Christianity to the "sexual level." Rather, it is a matter of *fully receiving* Christ's "descent into the flesh" so that that flesh can fully "ascend into the Trinity."

It's precisely through this divine descent "in the flesh" and human ascent "of the flesh" into the Trinity that the sexual relationship (that is, the relationship of man and woman consummated maritally in the two becoming one flesh) is restored in its full dignity and splendor as the primordial icon in creation of the "great mystery" of Christ's relationship with the Church. Applying this iconography as it is given by God in its integral goodness is not a matter of "sexualizing" Christianity. It is a matter of recognizing what Christianity already *is*: a "great mystery" that "clothes itself" in the splendid "wedding garment" provided by the primordial sacrament (marriage). Oh how beautiful this royal and mysterious "wedding garment" is! And oh how important to our salvation! Between here and the Marriage Feast of heaven, Christ tells us that we must all "put it on"—that is, we must remove all our soiled garments, and take this immaculate "wedding garment" to ourselves (see CCC 1682). We must be *clothed* by it and in it; we must *enter into* its mystery and be *transformed* by it. For, according to Christ's own seemingly harsh words, if we try to enter the heavenly celebration without this "wedding garment," we shall be bound "hand and foot" and cast "into the outer darkness" (see Mt 22:11-14).

The Danger of Manichaeism

Like those who struggle to see the beauty and holiness of the Mass because they've been (de)formed by diabolic mockeries of the liturgy, we often struggle to see the beauty and holiness of our sexuality because we've been (de)formed by diabolic mockeries of the body. We have been "estranged" in the modern world, as John Paul said, "from the 'great mystery' spoken of by the apostle [in Ephesians 5]" (LF 19). In place of this, the modern world has embraced that body-soul split typical of both Cartesian rationalism and Manichaeism (see LF 19). In short, if we are to understand and live the truth of our sexuality in Christ, we must continually contend with the "deep seated habits" that stem from Manichaeism in our way of thinking and evaluating things (see TOB 46:1). And it is precisely the "great mystery" of Ephesians 5, John Paul II tells us, which "radically frees our way of thinking from Manichaean elements" (TOB 117b:2).

Mani, or Manichaeus, after whom this heresy is named, condemned the body and all things sexual because he saw in the material world the source of evil (see TOB 45). In John Paul II's terms, he placed an "anti-value" on the physical world, on the body and sexuality. In Manichaean thinking, "matter is, at root, concupiscence, an evil appetite for pleasure . . . comparable if not identical with sexual desire, with 'libido'" (TOB 44:5, note 53). We are so influenced by these negative views of the body and sexuality—by these "anti-values"—that the "unaccustomed ear," John Paul observes, may think the tenets of Manichaeism harmonize with the teaching of the Gospel (see TOB 44:6). Indeed, we often confuse the two.

Of course, theologians who pride themselves in their orthodoxy—myself included—are loathe to admit to any heretical tendencies in their thinking. But claiming one is free from all hints of Manichaeism is akin to claiming one is free from all hints of original sin. Indeed, the

Manichaean tendency to "blame" or "accuse" the body goes as deep in us as does the shame we feel as the result of original sin.

In the beginning, John Paul tells us, "nakedness did not express a lack, but represented the full acceptance of the body in its whole human and thus personal truth." Furthermore, the "original acceptance of the body was in some sense the basis of the acceptance of the whole visible world" (TOB 27:3). Tragically, after original sin, the shame we now feel, "which shows itself without a doubt in the 'sexual' order," John Paul observes, also "reveals a *specific difficulty in sensing the human essentiality of one's own body*" (TOB 28:2). In other words, it is precisely the effect of original sin in us that makes it so difficult to embrace our bodiliness and sexuality. Sometimes, because of the difficulty of "being a body" in a fallen world, we can even take mistaken comfort in the faulty notion that we are "spiritual beings" housed for a time in the body. And, rather than face the disorder of our hearts, we tend to "blame" the body and the sexual difference itself for our problems. From within this frame, the logical solution to our problems becomes—subtly or sometimes not so subtly—to negate, repress, or otherwise devalue the body, especially its sexuality. Distancing ourselves from our sexuality keeps us "safe" . . . so we think. But it never takes us to the real cause of the problem.

As John Paul states, "With his shame about his own nakedness, the man seeks to cover the true origin of fear by indicating the effect so as not to name the cause" (TOB 27:1). In other words, the fig leaves are (quite literally) the original "cover-up." Covering the body indicates *the effect* of the original sin, but it doesn't get to *the cause* of it: the disordered desires of our own hearts. Like Adam, we don't want to admit to ourselves or to God what's really going on. We want to shift the blame from our own hearts to something else—to our own body, or, *to the other body-person*: "The woman whom you put here with me—she gave me the fruit . . . " (Gen 3:12). But this is the original "excuse" not to face the disorder of the heart. And this shifting of blame is "Manichaean" in its very essence. Indeed, as John Paul observes, "the essential error of the Manichaean ethos consists precisely in this" (TOB 45:4)—that is, in this shifting of blame from the heart to the body.

In heeding Christ's words never to "look lustfully," we must be very careful that we do not blame or reject the body itself (ours or someone else's). Indeed, it is much easier to blame the body than it is to examine our own hearts and seek "a full purification" (TOB 116:3): *If so-and-so weren't so beautiful . . .* or, *If so-and-so didn't dress that way . . . I wouldn't be lusting.* It may well be the case that "so-and-so" should dress more modestly, and both men and women should certainly take care to do so. Still, in the end, the *real* problem with lust is with oneself. Hence, when we are tempted to lust, we should not cast blame on the person who occasions it, but seek greater mastery of our own responses. As John Paul II observes, shifting the blame to the other person "would signify—perhaps not in a fully conscious way—a certain acceptance of the Manichaean 'anti-value.' It would not constitute a real and deep victory over the evil of the act [of lust]" (TOB 45:4). In fact, such an approach "might—and may always be—a loophole to avoid the requirements set in the Gospel" (TOB 44:6), that is, the requirements of ongoing growth and inner transformation. In practice, we're often drawn toward this Manichaean "loophole" because of sloth, understood as resentment of the fact that achieving the true good is difficult.

John Paul expresses the essential difference between the Manichaean and Christian mentalities as follows. While the Manichaean mentality places an "anti-value" on the body and sexuality, Christianity teaches that the body and sexuality "always remain a 'value not sufficiently appreciated'" (TOB 45:3). In other words, Manichaeism says "the body is bad" while Christianity says "the body is so good we have yet to fathom it." The Manichaean ethos is characterized by a *negation* of the value of the body and sex (blaming or rejecting the body because of lust), while "Christian ethos is characterized by *a transformation of the human person's conscience and attitudes . . . such as to express and realize the value of the body and sex* according to the Creator's original plan" (TOB 45:3). Alleluia! This is good news! However, if we wish to enter into this "transformation" and reclaim our sexuality according to God's original plan, we must prepare ourselves for an intense spiritual battle.

The Spiritual Battle

I do not think it is a coincidence that St. Paul follows his teaching on the "great mystery" in Ephesians 5 with a call to take up arms in the "great battle" in Ephesians 6. For the truth about man and woman and their life-giving union places us "at the center of the great struggle between good and evil, between life and death, between love and all that is opposed to love" (LF 23). Indeed, when spouses "unite as husband and wife, they . . . find themselves in the situation in which *the powers of good and evil fight against each other*" (TOB 115:2).

Is it any surprise, then, that the first thing St. Paul says we must do to arm ourselves for battle is to gird our loins with the truth (see Eph 6:14)? This is what John Paul II's TOB is: a clarion call for Christians (and the whole world) to gird their loins with the truth in order to reclaim our sexuality for Christ and the Church and, in this way, prepare ourselves for the eternal Marriage of the Lamb. As we observed at the start of this chapter, that's why the Enemy is literally hell-bent on mocking our sexuality: it's a very effective way of blinding us to the "great mystery" of Christ and the Church. Indeed, if we want to know what is most sacred in this world, all we need do is look to that which is most violently profaned. As I wrote in my book *Heaven's Song*:

> Lucifer is the great plagiarizer. He takes what belongs to Christ and puts his own name on it, claiming the erotic realm for himself. Tragically, it seems many Christians are content to let him have it. It is not uncommon to encounter people who—in the name of a supposed "piety"—find the very idea of linking erotic love and Christ's love unconscionable. In adopting this attitude, however, we do not overcome the deceiver's lies; we unwittingly buy into them. *We must not*

> *surrender the erotic realm to the enemy!* We *must not* let his distortions bind us to our own lusts and blind us to the "great mystery" revealed through our bodies! Precarious as it is, we *must* be courageous in reclaiming the erotic sphere for Christ and his Church. For, as both Old and New Testaments teach us—and as we see especially in the Song of Songs [and Ephesians 5]—the erotic sphere is the privileged realm of a divine revelation.
>
> Reclaiming the erotic sphere for Christ does not mean, of course, that we bring eros back "as is" from the enemy's turf. Rightly do the pious recoil at this idea. For appealing to the lustful distortions of our sexuality as images of the divine would be blasphemy. Rather, in the process of reclaiming the erotic realm for Christ, we must submit all that is "erotic" to a radical transformation. This process of transformation is an uncertain and fragile journey, but it is one made possible by grace. (HS, p. 13)

John Paul II spoke to this need to reclaim the erotic realm as follows: "It is necessary continually to rediscover the spousal meaning of the body and the true dignity of the gift in what is 'erotic.' This is the task of the human spirit . . . If one does not assume this task, the very attraction of the senses and the passion of the body can stop at mere concupiscence, deprived of all ethical value." If man stops here, he "does not experience that fullness of 'eros,' which implies the upward impulse of the human spirit toward what is true, good, and beautiful, so that what is 'erotic' also becomes true, good, and beautiful" (TOB 48:1).

And if we stop at lust, it becomes virtually impossible for us to see the body and sexuality as a "sign" that reveals the Mystery hidden in God from eternity (see TOB 40:4). Lust, in this case, darkens the intellect and blinds us to the glory revealed in the body and its members. In turn, we tend to project our own shame and distorted views on to those who *do* see something of the body's glory and are trying to help others to see the same.[48] Those who hold the heart in suspicion in this way continue to speak primarily of the "dangers" of sexuality and the "necessity of sin" in this sphere. They become "experts in the law," but they "take away the key to knowledge"—the key found, as so many saints attest, precisely in the Song of Songs and Ephesians 5. Restricted by lust, they don't know how to enter into the knowledge of the "great mystery" themselves, and they hinder those who are trying to enter (see Lk 11:52).

The Way of the Interior Life

For those who wish to enter the "private chambers" of the Song of Songs (see 1:4), that place of intimate union with the King, John Paul tells us that the path has been clearly laid out "by the teaching, so often found in the writings on the interior life and on mystical experience, about the three stages involved in 'following Christ' . . . the purgative way, the illuminative way, and the unitive way" (MI, p. 28). Unfortunately, these classic stages of spiritual growth are little known to Christians today, or, if known, they're often assumed to apply only to "extraordinary" Christians. John Paul II insists that this is the threefold way "along which Christ calls everyone" (MI, p. 28).

In the first stage, we learn with the help of grace and through much purgation to resist sin and observe the commandments. As we gain a certain proficiency, we progress into the illuminative way. Here, if we persevere through various trials, John Paul tells us, "we feel less and less burdened by the struggle against sin, and we enjoy more and more the divine light which pervades all of creation" (MI, p. 29). In turn, as we advance on the journey—which always involves deeper purification and illumination—we enter into "transforming union" with Christ. At this stage, as John Paul observes, "Created things cease to be a danger for us as once they were, particularly while we were still at the purgative stage of our journey. Creation, and other people in particular, not only regain their true light, given to them by God the Creator, but, so to speak, they lead us to God himself, in the way that he willed to reveal himself to us: as Father, Redeemer, and Spouse" (MI, p. 30).

In his "pastoral plan" for the new millennium, John Paul invited the whole Church to make this mystical journey into "nuptial union" with Christ. He even stated that we "have a duty" to show the world "to what depths the relationship with Christ can lead." It is "a journey totally sustained by grace," John Paul wrote, "which nonetheless demands an intense spiritual commitment and is no stranger to painful purifications (the 'dark night'). But it leads, in various possible ways, to the ineffable joy experienced by the mystics as 'nuptial union.' How can we forget here, among the many shining examples, the teachings of St. John of the Cross and St. Teresa of Avila?" (NMI 33).

We might do well to ask ourselves how "in tune" we are with John Paul II's "pastoral plan" for the new millennium. As a teacher of the faith, I must regularly ask myself: Am I inviting others on the mystical journey towards "nuptial union" with Christ? Am I persevering on that journey myself? When painful trials expose my brokenness and reveal my true poverty, how do I respond? Sometimes it can be uncomfortable even to frame the Gospel invitation in terms of "nuptial union" with the Lord. Why is that? Are there painful or dark experiences in my past that prevent me from seeing the holiness of the body and of sexual love in God's plan? Have I, perhaps, "blamed" the body and sexuality for some of these experiences?

God is a patient and gentle "counselor," like my friend who counsels those coming out of the pain and darkness of mock-liturgies. He knows where we have been, where we are, and where we must proceed on our journey. Indeed every one of us is in need of a deeper conversion of heart if we are to "see" the body, ours and our neighbor's, "*according to* God" (see CCC 2519). Hence, as Pope Benedict assures us, the Lord, in his great and merciful love for us, "continues to knock gently at the doors of our hearts and slowly opens our eyes if we open our doors to him" (JN2, p. 276). Let us open wide our doors to Christ!

Chapter 6

THE NARROW GATE BETWEEN IDOLATRY AND ICONOCLASM

The whole point of [icons] is to lead us beyond what can be apprehended at the merely material level, to awaken new senses in us, and to teach us a new kind of seeing, which perceives the Invisible in the visible.

—Joseph Cardinal Ratzinger (SL, p. 133)

As the result of original sin, John Paul II observes that it's as if man has "experienced a specific *fracture of the personal integrity of his own body, particularly in that which determines its sexuality*" (TOB 28:4). Ever since, we have found it very difficult to embrace the truth of the body as "image of God." This difficulty manifests itself in two polarized (and polarizing) errors: that of *idolatry* (the worship of images) on the one hand, and that of *iconoclasm* (the destruction of images) on the other. Let us explore this line of thinking as a way of illuminating some of the challenges that exist in reclaiming the body for the new evangelization.

As Christians, of course, we must diligently resist any tendency to worship the body.[49] With equal diligence, we must also resist any tendency to devalue, negate, or downplay the importance of the body. Again we find ourselves needing to balance what appear to be two "competing" truths. The gateway into the "fullness of truth" lies, as always, in the center point between these two extremes. To be sure, it is a "narrow gate." Whereas the gateway that veers off either towards idolatry or iconoclasm is "wide and broad" (Mt 7:13-14). Oh how easy it is to slip in either direction! And when we realize our error (speaking from experience) we usually tend toward the other imbalance and the narrow gate continues to elude us.

Striving to enter through the narrow gate means committing ourselves to a continual purification of our tendencies to idolatry and iconoclasm. The more we are purified of both, the closer we are to that "vortex" in the center that draws us up *bodily* into the divine Mystery with all the elemental force of Christ's Ascension and Mary's Assumption. Of course, here on earth we are still waiting for Christ to "transfigure our lowly bodies to be like his glorious body" (Phil 3:21). But even in our historical existence, the "vortex" of the narrow gate can lift us up "to the ineffable joy experienced by the mystics as 'nuptial union'" (NMI 33). "This union," John Paul tells us, "is realized in contemplation of the divine Being and in the experience of love which flows from it with growing intensity. In this way we somehow anticipate what is destined to be ours in eternity, beyond death and the grave" (MI, p. 39).

Icon vs. Idol

Icons, as they say in the theological tradition of the East, are "windows to heaven." They are *sacred images* inasmuch as they serve the "sacramental" purpose of "making visible what is invisible: the spiritual and the divine" (TOB 19:4). "The icon is venerated not for its own sake," John Paul II tells us, "but points beyond to the subject which it represents" (LA 7). Indeed, the "whole point" of iconography, the future Pope Benedict wrote, "is to lead us beyond what can be apprehended at the merely material level, to awaken new senses in us, and to teach us a new kind of seeing, which perceives the Invisible in the visible. The sacredness of the image consists precisely in the fact that it comes from an interior vision and thus leads us to such an interior vision" (SL, p. 133).

And here we can see that our understanding of the sacred image or "icon" is rife with implications for our understanding of the theology of our own bodies. We can (and should) expand the idea of "iconography" to include not just the sacred art of man, but the sacred art of God—his creation. As we discussed earlier, all of creation is "sacramental" inasmuch as it proclaims the glory of God. And at the crown of creation we find man, male and female, in the divine image. The human body in its original glory as male and female (that is, in its sexuality) is the primordial *icon*—given to us by God himself—of his own divine Mystery (see TOB 19:4).

And this is what the first man and woman *saw* when they looked at each other: they *saw* "the glory of God in the human body" (TOB 57:3). In this "seeing," according to John Paul II, the first man and woman experienced a holy kind of "fascination" with each other's bodies (see TOB 108:5,6; 117b:4)[50] because they saw the body not just as a physical object, but as a transparent sign of the whole mystery of the other as a "person" made in the divine image and called to love through the "sincere gift of self" (see TOB 13:1; 49:5). And this is what enabled them to be "naked without shame" (Gen 2:25): they *saw* and *honored* the sacred "iconography" of the body—which is to say, they *saw* and *honored* the full implications of the spousal meaning of their bodies.

We all know, of course, that this nakedness "without shame" did not last very long. Because of the tragedy of original sin, we all experience "a specific limitation of vision through the eyes of the body" (TOB 13:1). To the degree that concupiscence dominates our spiritual senses, it reduces our perception to the physical senses alone. As a result, we've almost lost the ability to see and honor the sacred "iconography" of the body.[51] In turn, our yearning for Infinite Beauty (for God) tends to get *stuck* on the "sign." To the degree that this happens, the icon becomes our "god"; the *icon* becomes an *idol*. In other words, when we idolize the body, we become so fixated on the "window to heaven" (the icon) that we fail to enter into the heavenly Mystery to which the window is meant to open us. "Claiming to be wise," we "exchange the glory of the immortal God for images." In turn, God gives us up "in the lust of [our] hearts to impurity" (see Rom 1:22-24).

From Idolatry to Iconoclasm

Towards the end of the first millennium, veneration of sacred images had become exaggerated and veered off into idolatry. Imbalance breeds imbalance, and the imbalanced response to this idolatry was to destroy the images: "iconoclasm."[52] The Church intervened at the Second

Council of Nicaea, insisting that icons should neither be adored nor destroyed. Instead, we must be invited back to the *new* way of "seeing" which the disciples experienced in Emmaus: "And their eyes were opened and they recognized him" (Lk 24:31). This is a "seeing" made possible not only with the "eyes of the body," but also with the "eyes of the heart" (see TOB 109:1).

Without this new way of seeing, physical realities become opaque and we find ourselves imprisoned by the limitations of the scientifically verifiable. From within this prison, we lean either in the direction of worshiping the physical world as *idolaters,* or rejecting the physical world as *iconoclasts.* The full-blown idolater views sensual pleasures as man's be-all and end-all and dives in head-first. The full-blown iconoclast views all that is sensual with suspicion and flees into a "safe" dis-incarnate "spirituality." The idolater seeks his comfort in "mere flesh." The iconoclast in "mere spirit." Neither has entered the realm of "incarnation"—the unity of flesh and spirit which God established "in the beginning," which sin rent asunder, and which Christ restores through his own glorious Incarnation.

Recall, as previously quoted, that the object of Catholic education, according to John Henry Newman, "is to reunite things which were in the beginning joined together by God and have been put asunder by man" (SP, sermon I). Christians are disintegrated creatures just like everyone else, but, if they are serious about their faith, they have committed themselves to the long and painful journey of interior re-integration. As we observed previously, for the sake of self-knowledge and further growth, it's important that we recognize in which direction we tend to lean. It's almost inevitable that we will oscillate between idolatry and iconoclasm in search of that narrow gate, that "vortex" that draws us up like reverse gravity into the Mystery of *bodily* participation in the divine life.

The Christian life is a journey "from the visible to the invisible, from the sign to the thing signified" (CCC 1075). But neither the idolater nor the iconoclast is letting the sign do its job of leading him in this way. The idolater is fixated on the sign, whereas the iconoclast imagines himself able to do without it.[53] The idolater says, "Keep your 'spirituality' away from my image" while the iconoclast says, "Keep your image away from my 'spirituality.'" And each is (understandably) put off by the other. For each is upholding a certain truth that remains unrecognized and unaffirmed by the other, and this makes each keen to point out the other's blind spot—usually while failing to acknowledge one's own.

Both Have Religious Motives

Iconoclasm "derived its passion in part from truly religious motives, from the undeniable dangers of a kind of adoration of the image" (SL, p. 120). But we can also recognize in this context that idolatry too derives in part from "truly religious motives." As St. Paul said to the men of Athens, having "looked carefully" at all their idols: "I see that in every way you are very religious" (Acts 17:22-23).

The idolatry Paul encountered in Athens was probably not much different than the idolatry of today. Statues and monuments of a pornographic nature were prevalent in Greek culture at the time (imagine if they had had photography). This may explain why Paul was "deeply distressed" upon seeing their idols (see Acts 17:16). Still, he did not overreact; he did not go from one imbalance to the other. Rather, having examined the situation "carefully" (Acts 17:23), he very creatively used their idolatry as a "meeting place" to lead the Athenians to Christ (see Acts 17:16-32). For, as Paul knew well, behind every idol is the human desire for the true God gone awry. Untwist the idolatry (which, of course, involves a lifetime of ongoing conversion), and we will eventually be shot like a rocket from the image toward the Reality it images, from created beauty toward divine Beauty itself—the true object of our every desire and attraction.

And so we can see that St. Paul, before issuing any condemnation of the Athenians' idolatry, offers an olive branch, an affirmation of that element of truth that he sees even in their pornographic distortions—if this was, indeed, the kind of idolatry he encountered in Athens. We should learn how to follow Paul's lead here and—before condemning the modern "cult of the body"—learn how to affirm the element of truth hidden within it. If we don't do this, or find that we "can't" do this, chances are we will lean towards a rejection of the image, or, in this case, an eschewing or negative evaluation of the human body.

Here we can see the meeting point between the errors of iconoclasm and Manichaeism. If our approach to the imbalance of idolizing the body in any way "blames" the body, negates the body, or otherwise devalues it, this approach "would signify—perhaps not in a fully conscious way—a certain acceptance of the Manichaean 'anti-value.' It would not constitute a real and deep victory over the evil of the act, which is evil . . . of a spiritual nature" (TOB 45:4). In other words, the problem with idolizing the body lies not with the body; it lies in the human heart. It's a spiritual problem. Hence, the real solution to the problem is not found in distancing oneself from the body. The solution lies in a proper "*ethos of seeing*" (TOB 63:6). It lies in that "new ethos" of the Gospel that affords a "*transformation of the human person's conscience and attitudes*" enabling us "*to express and realize the value of the body and sex* according to the Creator's original plan" (TOB 45:3). And the Creator's original plan is that the body would be an icon of his own Invisible Mystery. Oh, Lord, open our eyes![54]

Idolaters Are Far Too Easily Pleased

Idolatry "remains a constant temptation to faith," the *Catechism* tells us (CCC 2113). Why? It seems to have something to do with the very nature of sacramental reality. God created all the sensual pleasures of this earth—the deliciousness of food and drink, the profound intensity of sexual union, the glories of music, the breathtaking beauty of nature, to name a few—as so many "icons" of his own Mystery. In a very real way, sensual pleasures—the pleasures we experience through our senses—provide (or are *meant* to provide) a "foretaste" of heaven, a small "glimmer" of God's extravagant goodness. But precisely because these icons can provide a *taste* of heaven, there is a "constant temptation" to treat them *as* "heaven"—that is, to idolize them.

It would seem that the idolater essentially lacks patience. He doesn't want to wait for the fulfillment of heaven, nor receive it from the Lord's hands as he intends. Instead, the idolater wants to "take hold of" the satisfaction of his heart's desire here and now. Heaven, of course, is out of reach, so he turns to the next best thing: icons of heaven that are within reach. "Wait for the Lord; be strong, and let your heart take courage; yes, wait for the Lord!" (Ps 27:14). "Take delight in the Lord, and he will grant you the desires of your heart" (Ps 37:4).

Iconoclasm, while an understandable *human* response to idolatry, makes the fundamental error (just like Manichaeism and so many other heresies) of "blaming" the physical realm for the problem. Iconoclasm directs the heart's discontent with "false worship" towards the object worshiped falsely, assuming that destroying or negating that object will somehow solve the problem. But *the problem is not with the physical world* (it never is!). The problem is not with the body or the senses or the pleasure of the body via the senses. The problem is with the stilted desires of the human heart. When we fall prey to idolatry, we're not filled with "too much" desire, but *too little—far* too little. If we were truly consumed with desire for the Infinite, we would never be deceived into thinking finite things could satisfy. As C. S. Lewis put it:

> Indeed, if we consider the unblushing promises of reward and the staggering nature of the rewards promised in the Gospels, it would seem that our Lord finds our desires, not too strong, but too weak. We are half-hearted creatures, fooling about with drink and sex and ambition when infinite joy is offered us, like an ignorant child who wants to go on making mud pies in a slum because he cannot imagine what is meant by the offer of a holiday at the sea. We are far too easily pleased. (*The Weight of Glory*, p. 26)

From Idolatry to "True Worship"

The operation of divine grace affords the only true solution to idolatry—a healing of the heart that "untwists" what sin has "twisted" so we can see what we truly desired all along: the infinite joy of union with the divine. But we must commit to cooperating with this grace by persevering along the threefold way of the interior life—the way of purgation, illumination, and union.

This journey involves an "undeniably painful transformation 'as through fire,'" as Pope Benedict XVI put it (SS 47). But as we humbly endure this painful fire, our idols lose their allure. "Created things cease to be a danger for us as once they were, particularly while we were still at the purgative stage of our journey. Creation, and other people in particular, not only regain their true light, given to them by God the Creator, but, so to speak, they lead us to God himself, in the way that he willed to reveal himself to us: as Father, Redeemer, and Spouse" (MI, p. 30). In other words, to the degree that our hearts are transformed and redirected from creatures to their Creator, our idols become for us what they always have been in reality—so many icons that "lead us to God himself." In this way, our "false worship" is transformed into "true worship." As I wrote in *Heaven's Song*:

> We worship that which we think will satisfy our deepest hunger. In his first commandment, then—"You shall have no other gods before me . . . " (Dt 5:7)—God is simply saying: "I am your satisfaction; I, and I alone, can satisfy your

hunger." As the psalmist puts it, "You shall not bow down to a foreign god. I am the Lord your God . . . Open your mouth wide, and I will fill it" (Ps 81:9-10). Our world worships the body, worships sex. Why? Because so many of us have come to believe that sexual union will satisfy our deepest hunger. The world is on to something here. For marital union *is* meant to be an *icon* of our ultimate satisfaction. It's meant to point us to Christ. But when we worship the paint and the wood of a religious icon rather than letting it open a window to heaven, we stop short (far short!) of what we truly desire and the icon degenerates into an idol.

Isn't this what Christ is helping the thirsty Samaritan woman to understand? She had been trying to satisfy her thirst with six men, six being the imperfect biblical number. Jesus comes to her as her "seventh husband"—the perfect biblical number. Jesus presents himself to her as her perfect satisfaction. In his dialogue with her, it's as if he were saying: "I know you are thirsty for love, I know. But, my dearly beloved, you've been 'looking for love in all the wrong places . . . looking for love in too many faces.' *I'm the love you've been looking for!* If you only knew

> the gift of God . . . if you only knew the love that *I* wanted to give you . . . You would ask, and I would give it to you . . . and you would never thirst again. In fact, this love will well up in you to eternal life" (see Jn 4:10-14). That day, having found the "living water" of Christ, the Samaritan woman became a "true worshiper" (Jn 4:23). When we find that which truly satisfies our thirst and vulnerably surrender ourselves to it, then we are worshiping God "in spirit and in truth."
>
> In short, the Christian revolution transforms sexual union from something that *is worshiped* into something that *is worship*. When lived sacramentally and liturgically, spouses are not seeking ultimate satisfaction in their union. Rather, they find in their union a sign, a foreshadowing, of ultimate satisfaction. And in that sign, through that sign, they offer praise and worship *to God* with a living hope in the consummation of the Marriage of the Lamb. It is union with God—participation in the eternal bliss of the divine exchange—that alone satisfies the heart's thirst. (HS, pp. 129-130)

The key point here, as Father Jacques Philippe expresses, is that "one passion can only be cured by another—a misplaced love by a greater love, wrong behavior by right behavior that makes provisions for the desire underlying the wrongdoing, recognizes the conscious or unconscious needs that seek fulfillment and . . . offers them legitimate satisfaction" (IF, p. 113). This is why iconoclasm can never solve the problem of idolatry and idolatry can never solve the problem of iconoclasm. Whichever direction one is moving, the swing of the pendulum simply exchanges one wrong behavior for another.

Searching for the Balance

When we understand the body as a *theology*—an "icon" of the divine mystery—we want diligently to safeguard this icon against anything that even hints at a lack of appreciation for it, devaluation of it, or, worst of all, "iconoclastic" rejection of it. Since man is "'obliged to regard his body as good and to hold it in honor'" (CCC 364), rightly so, we become very sensitive to any language or line of thinking that even appears to negate or devalue the body. In our reaction against a kind of "iconoclasm" widespread among Christians today, we can sometimes push back too heavily at times. At other times, perhaps a hypersensitivity to "puritanism" can lead us to see a negation of the body where, in fact, there is none.

Conversely, when we understand that the soul reveals "that which is of greatest value" in us and makes us "most especially in God's image" (CCC 363), we want diligently to safeguard these truths against anything that even hints at "a neo-pagan notion that tends to promote the *cult of the body*" and "make it an absolute value" (CCC 2289). Rightly so, we become very sensitive to any language or line of thinking that even appears to promote or encourage the same idolatrous obsession with the body rampant in the culture. But in our reaction against this idolatry, we can push back too heavily at times. A hypersensitivity to idolatry can lead us to see it where, in fact, there is none.[55]

How should Christians respond to the secular world's "cult of the body"—with a de-emphasis on the body and a renewed emphasis on "the spirit"? If so, one might have expected John Paul II to respond to the sexual revolution by offering the Church and the world an extended "theology of the spirit." But, instead, he gave us an in-depth, theology *of the body*. Why? Can we not recognize in John Paul II's Theology of the Body—a gift bequeathed the Church at the end of the second millennium—that the Successor of Peter was applying the critical lessons bequeathed the Church towards the end of the first millennium in the iconoclastic crisis? To the world he was saying: we mustn't worship the body. To believers he was saying: we mustn't reject the body. To both he was saying: we must learn how to venerate the body as an icon of the divine mystery.

The Summation of All Heresies

Much is at stake in the way we choose to respond to our culture's idolatrous worship of sex. If we lean too far in the other direction, we will eventually fall into a hellish black hole that robs us of everything Christ and his Church offer us. For iconoclasm is "the summation of all heresies" as Cardinal Ratzinger observes. Indeed the Church has recognized it as such ever since she first confronted this error at the Second Council of Nicaea (see SL, p. 122).

But why the summation of *all* heresies? Because the antichrist is the one who denies Christ come in the flesh (see 1 Jn 4:2-3), and this is what iconoclasm does: it denies the Incarnation. We've already quoted Ratzinger's statement: "The Incarnation means, in the first place, that the invisible God enters into the visible world, so that we, who are bound to matter, can know him." The Incarnation is a "descent of God." It's "aimed at man's transformation through the Cross and to the new corporeality of the

Resurrection. God seeks us where we are, not so that we can stay there, but so that we can come to be where he is." Therefore, "this descent of God is intended to draw us into a movement of ascent" (SL, pp. 122-123).

But iconoclastic thinking doesn't really believe that this *ascent* "from the lower to the higher" is possible. Why? Because, despite all affirmations to the contrary, it hasn't fully embraced God's *descent* into the flesh. It remains suspicious of the "lower" reality of the body and the senses. For it holds them bound inextricably to concupiscence. It is certainly true that we experience within our bodies "a force that often undermines man" and our senses are "often urged or pushed, as it were, toward evil," as John Paul II says (TOB 72:4). But we must not think that the sensual life is fundamentally opposed to the spiritual life. As Caryll Houselander lyrically expressed it, "It is not in making our flesh unfeeling that we hallow God's name on earth, but in offering it to God burning with the flame of life" (RG, p. 105).

An Authentic Sensual Life

"The senses are not to be discarded," insists the future Pope Benedict. Rather, through the gift of redemption, "they should be expanded to their widest capacity." Only in light of the Incarnation "does it become clear that the senses belong to faith, that the new seeing does not abolish them, but leads them to their original purpose" (SL, p. 123). And that original purpose is to open us to the "mystical senses"—to seeing, hearing, smelling, tasting, touching, and feeling spiritual and divine mysteries.

It is in this way that we come to "taste and see" God's own goodness. This happens not by "skipping over" the physical senses, but, as our physical senses "expand to their widest capacity," all the glorious icons God has given us in the created world open their particular "window to heaven" and we rejoice to enter in. We come to "sense" God's mysterious presence *everywhere* and in *everything*, in all our creaturely, bodily experiences. That fundamental suspicion towards the body, the senses, and the physical world begins to evaporate. We remain aware that the risk of sin always exists, but we no longer think and speak of this world primarily in terms of sin. Our emphasis instead becomes the real possibility of freedom and virtue, which allow us to rejoice in the gifts of this world as so many foretastes of the joys that await us in heaven.

Don't we see this in Christ himself? Jesus must have thoroughly enjoyed good food and good wine. Why else would he have been accused of being "a glutton and a drunkard" (Lk 7:34)? Those blinded by their own "iconoclastic thinking" (which, again, is really just the flip side of idolatry) projected vice on to Christ's virtue. They couldn't imagine anything else in someone who took such delight in created pleasures. "No man ever enjoyed life as he did. He gathered up the color, sound, touch, meaning of everything about him and united it all to the most exquisite sensitiveness, the most pure capacity for delight" (RG, p. 101).

And those who follow Jesus through the purgative, illuminative, and unitive stages of the journey also gradually take on Christ's own "pure capacity for delight." They come to an exquisite appreciation of the many *icons* of the created world—without making *idols* of them. They experience deeply both the agony *and* the ecstasy of following Christ. This is the rich harvest we reap through a life of proper asceticism. Asceticism is not the *end,* but the *means.* A life of proper *fasting* bears fruit in a life of proper *feasting.*[56] A life of learning a proper "custody of the eyes" bears fruit in a proper "ethos of seeing." Returning to our previous example, the bishop who "looked away" can become the bishop who "sees" . . . *if* he perseveres on the interior journey of purification. To get there, as John Paul II wrote, a person

> must *learn* with perseverance and consistency *what* the meaning of the body *is,* the meaning of femininity and masculinity. He must learn it not only through . . . abstraction (though this is needed as well), but above all in the sphere of the interior reactions of his own "heart." This is a "science" that cannot really be learned only from books, because it consists primarily of deep knowledge of human interiority. [Deep in the heart] man learns to distinguish between what, on the one hand, makes up the manifold richness of masculinity and femininity in the signs that spring from their perennial call and creative attraction and what, on the other hand, bears only the sign of concupiscence. And although within certain limits these . . . inner movements of the heart can be confused with each other, . . . the inner man is *called by Christ to reach a more mature and complete evaluation that allows him to distinguish and judge the various movements of his own heart.* One should add that this task *can* be carried out and that it is truly worthy of man. (TOB 48:4)

Faith Collapses without Images We Can "See"

In the history of Christian theology, there has always been a creative tension represented by these terms (the meanings of which must be properly held together): mystery/sacrament; hidden/revealed; veiled/unveiled; unknowable/known; transcendent/immanent; intangible/tangible; invisible/visible. All these tensions are summarized in what the mystical tradition has called an "apophatic" approach to God and a "katophatic" one. The former stresses that God lies *infinitely beyond* all images and words (see CCC 42) while the latter recognizes that *we need* images and words as created beings in order to encounter the divine (see CCC 1146). As always, the two truths must be properly held together if we are to avoid error.

Benedict XVI observes that a "flight into a purely 'negative' (apophatic) theology" almost inevitably occurs when, influenced by a dualistic split between body and soul, "we can no longer apprehend the transparency of the spirit in the senses." Iconoclasm "rests ultimately on a one-sided apophatic theology, which recognizes only the Wholly Other-ness of God beyond all images and words." But if God cannot descend to our level and communicate himself through visible images, "faith collapses" (SL, pp. 123-124).

From this perspective, matter is "thought of as completely impervious to God, as mere matter, and thus deprived of its dignity." In turn—when we deprive matter of its dignity in this way—sensual, bodily realities come to be considered so "beneath" God that the very idea of using sensual, bodily imagery to convey divine mysteries becomes distasteful, even appalling. But we must be very careful here. For, as the future Pope Benedict observes, "What seems like the highest humility toward God turns into pride" (SL, pp. 123-124). Why pride? Because in such case we think we know what is best suited for God more than God does.

It is God who has ordained the human body and spousal love in all its original splendor as the primordial icon of his own ineffable mystery of Love and Communion. *It is God* who planted eros as a vehement flame within the human heart that's meant to lead us through all that is true, good, and beautiful to ultimate Truth, Goodness, and Beauty. Woe to us if we fearfully reject or repress eros, seeking to snuff it out in the name of "holiness." Woe to us if we deny, devalue, neglect, or otherwise reject human sexuality as an icon of the divine. Woe to us if we become iconoclasts. In doing so, we unwittingly buy in to the summation of all heresies and reject "*the foundation of the whole sacramental order*" (TOB 95b:7). By doing so we reject the very "window to heaven" that God has written into the order of creation.

Courage to Enter the Divine Fire

The idolater's problem is of a different nature. He's not fearfully repressing eros. He's recklessly indulging it. He's not rejecting the "window to heaven." He's so mesmerized by it that he can't see beyond it: the means have become the idolater's end.

What's needed of both the iconoclast and the idolater is the courage to follow the sign of the body into the divine reality it signifies; what's needed is the courage to bring all the distortions of eros into Christ's healing light so they can be "untwisted" and we can surrender ourselves to the full power of eros as God intends, following its rightful trajectory *the whole way* into the blazing fire of God's love, of God's Eros. And, oh, what a terrifying reality that can be! Great courage in desire is an absolute necessity along the path of "nuptial union" with the Lord and it's something for which we must earnestly pray.

Perhaps this explains in part why the "sinners and prostitutes" embraced Jesus more readily than did the Scribes and Pharisees. First, we must acknowledge that whether one errs on the side of idolatry or iconoclasm, following Christ always involves a long journey of conversion and a radical reorientation of one's life. And yet, as Aristotle wisely observed, the reckless person is closer to the virtue of courage than the fearful person (see NE, II.8).

As we saw earlier in Christ's discussion with the woman at the well, the distance between idolatry and "true worship" is not always as far as we tend to think, whereas the journey from iconoclasm to true worship seems not only longer, but also, in some ways, more difficult. For one thing, iconoclasm (and all its attendant errors) can more readily pass for religious "success," since we are prone to think—erroneously!—that rigorism in bodily matters equals holiness. The idolater, on the other hand, as the more apparent "sinner," may also be more aware of his own misery and need. As the parable of the tax collector and the Pharisee who "went up to the temple to pray" makes clear, things are not always as they seem in terms of who stands "justified" before God (see Lk 18:9-14). Father Raniero Cantalamessa observes that "the kingdom is offered first to publicans and prostitutes [not] because God favors their current states." Rather, "those people are capable of reformation, while the self righteous are not"

(BES)—unless, of course, they renounce the pride they take in their own "success."

Another cause for concern regarding iconoclasm is this: if the habits we form on earth create a trajectory for the life hereafter, what will a hardened iconoclast do, for example, when the "great sign" of the "woman clothed with the sun" appears and bids him to come to her embrace? It seems to me there is a danger that such a person would do what had become habitual in this life—reject the sign and turn away from it as if it were perverse. Father Simon Tugwell writes:

> A very important factor here is what we may call Christian spontaneity. It does not, perhaps, in the last analysis, matter all that much what you do with forethought; what really matters . . . is what you do without thinking . . . what you do when you do not have time to work out how to respond. It is this that will reveal what kind of person you are, and that is what is important. After all, the kingdom of heaven comes like a thief in the night (I Thess 5:2), with a suddenness which will not allow us to work out how we are going to react.
>
> The way the tree falls, so will it lie (Eccles 11:3). The way that it falls is certainly the result of a

long process; but its actual falling is a crisis that comes suddenly. There is quite a lot we can do in advance to determine how we shall fall, but all of it is but rehearsal for something we shall have to do instinctively when the time comes. This is why it is so important to take seriously St. Thomas' refusal to identify virtue with right action; so long as we have wrong desires, even if we do not give in to them, we are not yet virtuous. When it comes time for the final crunch . . . there may be no opportunity for second thoughts . . . We must unmuddy [our hearts] so that our spontaneity itself is transformed. (BSCT, p. 95)

Chapter 7

THE NEW EVANGELIZATION AND "THE WAY OF BEAUTY"

We must summon fresh energy for tackling the problem of how to announce the gospel anew in such a way that this world can receive it, and we must muster all of our energies to do this.

—Pope Benedict XVI (LW, p. 130)

Christopher Hitchens is one of the more popular atheist authors making his case in the public square against religious faith. I recently started reading his #1 *New York Times* bestseller *God Is Not Great: How Religion Poisons Everything*. This book had already been on my radar, since I try to remain aware of what the culture is saying, especially when it comes to religion. However, what pushed me over the edge to buy this vehement denunciation of religion was one of the blurbs on the back cover: "Many of the author's reproaches against believers of all religions . . . are well-founded, and must be taken seriously." Nothing surprising there, if such an endorsement were written by someone who shared Hitchens's disdain for religion. What commanded my attention was the fact that this statement was credited to Father Raniero Cantalamessa, the official Preacher to the Papal Household.

Knowing how comments can be misleading when taken out of context, I looked up the article from which this quote was excerpted for a more complete version of the statement. After expressing genuine gratitude to the person who sent him Hitchens's book, Cantalamessa states the following in the second paragraph:

> Many of the author's reproaches against believers of all religions—the book treats Islam no better than Christianity, which shows considerable courage on the part of the author—are well-founded, and must be taken seriously so that the same errors of the past are not repeated in the future. The Second Vatican Council states that the Christian faith can and should benefit even from the criticisms of its attackers, and this is certainly one of those cases. (cantalamessa.org/en/articolo)

As one would expect, the rest of the article provides a well-reasoned rebuttal to the main thrust of Hitchens's argument. Still, in his final paragraph the papal preacher states, "I repeat: one cannot fail to acknowledge the author's extraordinary erudition and the relevance of some of his criticisms." Here it seems we find a tacit indictment from a high-level Vatican personality—not of religious faith itself, obviously—but of *the way* certain people of faith believe or of *the way they represent* what they believe to others. And so we must wonder: if people are "tuning out" when we share the Gospel, it might not be their problem. It might be ours.

In Chapter I we looked briefly at "the great task we face" in bringing the Gospel within the horizon of the secular world's understanding (see LW, p. 64). In this chapter we'll take a deeper look.

An Itinerary of Friendship with the Culture

In a document entitled *Via Pulchritudinis,* which means "the way of beauty," the Pontifical Council for Culture summarized well the cultural challenges facing the Church today:

> The culture emerging from a materialist and atheistic worldview, characteristic of secularized societies, causes disaffection from religion, sometimes opposition to it, particularly Christianity, with a new anti-Catholicism. Many

> live as though God did not exist, as though his presence and his Word had no influence on the life of people and societies. They struggle to affirm clearly their religious belonging, and their spirituality remains in the strict domain of their private lives. Religious experience is often disassociated from a clear belonging to an ecclesial institution: some believe without belonging, others belong without offering visible signs of their believing. (VP I)

This clearly underlines the need "for a new apostolic thrust by the Church to evangelize cultures with an effective inculturation of the Gospel" (VP I). How does the Church seek to accomplish this? She "examines the *signs of the times* and draws pointers from them to develop 'bridges' which lead to a meeting with the God of Jesus Christ through an itinerary of friendship in a dialogue of truth" (VP II). As a biblical example of this "itinerary of friendship in a dialogue of truth," we're reminded again of Paul's dialogue with the Athenians in which the Apostle "strives to adapt himself to the mentality of his audience," as John Paul II once put it (BNA, p. 159).

If the health of marriage and family life serves as a barometer for measuring the success of evangelization, we must acknowledge that Christians, by and large, have not been effective witnesses to the Gospel in the last few generations. I think this demands that those who claim to have the "fullness of the Gospel"—namely, Catholics who believe and affirm all that the Church believes and affirms—ask themselves some hard questions. Does the average "orthodox Catholic" even know how to enter into "an itinerary of friendship in a dialogue of truth" with those who have shaped and continue to shape our secularized culture? If we had the opportunity to sit down, say, with President Obama or Lady Gaga, what would we say to them? Would our message and demeanor attract them or turn them away? Would we know how to look into their eyes and communicate a heartfelt love? Do we even have a heartfelt love for such people? Would we be able to show them—really *show them*—genuine compassion, understanding, and human respect?

Today's cultural situation demonstrates with swelling urgency the need for Catholics and all believers to "go into the main streets and invite everyone to the wedding feast" (Mt 22:9). But no one from "main street" will come if we don't put the invitation in a language they can connect with and understand. Jesus attracted people from all walks of life when he preached, but he seemed to have a particular love for and ability to reach the "tax collectors and prostitutes." He even insisted that they would enter the kingdom ahead of the elders, scholars, and religious elites (see Mt 21:28-32). It seems we, too, should have a particular love for and interest in reaching such people if we are to be "in tune" with Jesus's approach.

The Frustration of St. Francis Xavier

In discussions about how best to reach the culture with the Gospel, a certain tension often exists between academic theologians and those with a more popularly accessible approach to teaching the faith. In the Office of Readings on the feast of St. Francis Xavier, the Church invites us to reflect on a letter this great missionary saint wrote from India in which he permits himself to vent a bit to St. Ignatius of Loyola:

> Many, many people hereabouts are not becoming Christians for one reason only: there is nobody to make them Christians. Again and again I have thought of going around the universities of Europe, especially Paris, and everywhere crying out like a madman, riveting the attention of those with more learning than charity: "What a tragedy: how many souls are being shut out of

> heaven and falling into hell, thanks to you!" I wish they would work as hard at [reaching these souls] as they do at their books, and so settle their account with God for their learning and the talents entrusted to them.[57]

The report from "main street" is *dire.* It's a pornographic culture of death out there—a war zone. Grenades are exploding everywhere. People are missing limbs. Torsos have been shredded by shrapnel. And countless people are being left to die in the dust for the simple fact that we have not found a way to reach them. Clearly, there must be a place for Catholics to "talk amongst themselves" and for academic theologians to debate the "finer points" of theology with their very refined, nuanced language. Surely a great many saints spoke with sophisticated terminology. However, if in the end the language we use has created a Catholic "bubble" with no easy way out and no easy way in, sharing the Gospel with the secular world becomes impossible.[58]

Pope Paul VI wrote that "all of us who feel the spur of the apostolate should examine closely the kind of speech we use. Is it easy to understand? Can it be grasped by ordinary people? Is it current idiom?" An effective teacher of the Faith "is always at pains to learn the sensitivities of his audience, and if reason demands it, he adapts himself and the manner of his presentation to the susceptibilities and the degree of intelligence of his hearers" (ES 81). Indeed, as Paul VI insisted, "we must forgo all privilege and the use of unintelligible language, and adopt the way of life of ordinary people in all that is human and honorable . . . if we wish to be listened to and understood. Then, before speaking, we must take great care to listen not only to what men say, but more especially to what they have it in their hearts to say. Only then," concluded Paul VI, "will we understand them and respect them, and even, as far as possible, agree with them" (ES 87).

The Sacred and the Secular

Insular thinking and living often leads us to construct a strict divide between the "sacred" and the "secular." We conclude that the sacred lies *here* and "holy people" talk like *this,* while the secular lies *way over there* and "unholy people" talk like *that.* But is this a truly Catholic way of seeing the world? There is a valid distinction to make between the sacred and the secular, but there needn't be—and from the Christian point of view, shouldn't be—a divide. Christ is the definitive bridge.

Secular comes from the Latin root *saeculum* which simply means "the present world" or "the present time." The Incarnation is God's willingness to meet us *in* "the present world"—right "where we are," as Cardinal Ratzinger put it. The Ultimate Sacred *descends* into our "secular" world, "not so we can stay there, but so that we can come to be where he is" (SL, p. 123), so that we can *ascend* with him. And in this *ascent,* the "secular" is not left behind. Rather, all that is authentically human ascends with us so it can be transformed and perfected.

Archbishop Ravasi, President of the Pontifical Council for Culture, explains that when we recognize the proper bridge between the sacred and the secular (rather than a divide), "we are brought to envisage a certain number of other distinctions which are no longer indices of exclusivity or separation, notably 'world/Church,' 'reason/faith,' and 'nature/grace' or 'natural/supernatural' and "temporal/spiritual' . . . In comparison with these distinct but not opposing realities, the risk of a total separation can appear, or of hostility and conflict that can result in one trying to dominate the other." But this is not the Catholic way. Thus, considering the Church's relationship to the secular world, Ravasi concludes, "Let us resolutely say that we wish to be closer to the secular world in which we are already immersed in many ways, and which we do not fear to say we love and embrace, albeit with a certain amount of discernment" (*L'Osservatore Romano,* July 30, 2008, p. 9).

Culture Is Not Totally Corrupted

In our evangelical efforts, we can draw a certain analogy with the Incarnation itself. We could put it like this: like Christ, we must be willing to "descend" into the culture so we can help the culture "ascend." In Chapter I we quoted Pope Benedict's statement that "one has to meet one's listeners halfway, one has to speak to them in terms of their own horizon. But at the same time our task is to open up this horizon, to broaden it, and turn our gaze toward the ultimate" (LW, p. 179). We certainly want to help the culture "ascend." But no one has ascended but he who descended (see Jn 3:13). And what does he ascended mean but that he first descended (see Eph 4:9)?

If we are to speak of "descending" into the culture, we must insist that this does not mean "holding our noses" while we quickly pluck people out of the cesspool. Since human nature is not totally corrupted (see CCC 405), neither is culture at large. Evil is not creative. It can only take what God has made—all of which is good—and twist it, distort it, or deprive it of its fullness. "Thus, in the Christian view," John Paul II tells us, evil "always, in some way, refers to a good" (SD 7). This is a critical point. We often give evil far too much credit, far too much weight, as if it were something that existed in its own right, as if it were something with ontological "is-ness." But this is the error, yet again, of Manichaean thinking. For Manichaeism expresses an "ontological principle of evil" (see TOB 44:6). In other words, it assigns to evil its own existence, a parallel world to the world of good. But, when existence is properly understood, an "ontological principle of evil" is an *ontological impossibility.*

Philosophically speaking, evil does not "exist." Obviously, that does *not* mean "there is no such thing as evil." It means, as John Paul II wrote, that "Christianity proclaims the essential *good of existence* and the good of that which exists" (SD 7). Since everything God created is good, "being and the good are convertible" (TOB 2:5). Hence, if something has "being," if something "exists" (in the philosophical sense of the term), *it is good.* Evil, therefore, does not "exist." It can only be "a certain lack, limitation, or distortion of good" (SD 7). Evil is real, to be sure. But it is not something positive. It is a real *privation* of what is meant to be there. Evil is like cold or darkness. Neither "exist." What exists are heat and light. Cold and darkness are their absence.

As we let the fundamental truth about good and evil sink in more and more deeply, it changes our whole approach to evil. We overcome it not by categorically "throwing it out." Why not? Because there is *always* a baby in that bathwater. We overcome evil with good, as Scripture says (see Rom 12:21). That is, we overcome evil by "filling in the void" it leaves, or by "untwisting the good" it distorts. We must let this truth become a living foundation for us: all that exists is good . . . very good; and sin has not cancelled that out. As we learn to *rest* in this truth, we are no longer rankled by evil. We see it for what it is, and we are "at ease" with ourselves and the world—not because we have turned a blind eye to the horrors of evil, but because we are confident in the divine plan to overcome evil with good. We can maintain an interior peace even in the face of *great evil* because we know how to "let God be God" in dealing with evil, and we know how to participate *effectively* in his redemptive plan. We ultimately conquer evil not by wagging fingers at it, but by "suffering it" in union with Christ. That is, we conquer evil with mercy.

The Primacy of Mercy

All this leads to a peaceful acceptance of human freedom, even when we (or others) make mistakes in exercising it. For we know that the Father foresaw man's abuse of freedom and, before he even created us, made superabundant provision for it. "Where sin abounds, grace abounds *even more*" (Rom 5:20).

We often think the way to eradicate sin is to eradicate our ability to choose sin—but that would be to eradicate human freedom. Such a "solution" is human thinking, not divine. We can and should be at peace with human freedom, because, as Angelo Cardinal Scola wrote, from "within [the Church's] womb, it is possible to live the experience of a redeemed freedom, and thus a freedom which ultimately is no longer determined by the possibility of sin" (NM, p. 256). In our struggle with sin, especially when we've become unsettled interiorly by the reality of evil, we are often led to the question: *Why, God, did you give us freedom? If you didn't want us to sin, why did you make it possible for us to do so?* Cardinal Scola reflects:

> Why did God the Father create man so radically free? Because he was not afraid—if it is permitted to speak in such terms—of the eventuality of

> sin, of human freedom going astray. Because the Father creates us in Jesus Christ, the incarnate Son who died and is risen . . . [This means, right from the beginning] the eventuality of sin is already included in his gratuitous and merciful design. God creates us in mercy; created freedom is redeemed freedom in the sense that, in the eventuality of sin, forgiveness is already offered to it "in advance," as the ever renewed possibility of returning to the Father's house. (NM, p. 256)

Scola is quick to point out that none of this means that sin loses "the terrible character of an offense against God and a mortal wound." But the emphasis is not placed on man's sin. It's placed on the Father's loving plan of redemption. We must not consider man "in function of his sin, but in light of the redemption worked by Jesus Christ. Only thus is man truly free!" Scola exclaims. "Only the primacy of mercy allows us to contemplate our freedom with serenity, to see it as a positive fact and not as a threat or condemnation" (NM, p. 256).

Oh what liberation to see ourselves this way! And oh what liberation to see *others* this way, to see the whole world this way! And all of this has profound implications for evangelization. Evangelization should begin with an affirmation of humanity's fundamental and original goodness, rather than a declaration of our sinfulness. Of course, we must recognize our sinfulness, but we have no reference for knowing what sin even *is* without first recognizing the fundamental truth of human goodness. Many Protestant Reformers, with their declaration of man's "utter depravity," began to lose sight of this. In turn, when man's "utter depravity" is the starting point, the main goal of "evangelization" becomes convincing people that they are sinners in need of salvation. That's true, of course. We *are* sinners desperately in need of salvation. The Gospel is *always* a call to repentance (see Mt 4:17). But as witnesses to Christ, should "You are a sinner" be the first thing out of our mouths?

Almost inevitably, whether intended or not, this approach places the evangelist "above" the evangelee. The evangelist becomes the "saved" one who—having supposedly "figured life out"—is now in a position to render judgment on those who "haven't." Rarely is this intentional, but human pride often creeps in to our efforts to evangelize (I'm speaking from experience here). We can sometimes evangelize with a pretext of mercy, but underneath we're harboring a sense of superiority, judgment, and resentment towards "sinners." But how can we remove the speck in our brother's eye if we do not recognize the beam in our own?

The Primacy of Affirmation

The primary message and approach of Christian evangelization should rest on what we might call a "theology of affirmation." Such an approach knows well that we are sinners, but in order to place sin in its proper context, it proclaims first and foremost: it is *good to exist.* It is good to be here! (see Mt 17:4). It is good to be human. It is good to be created male and female. And it is good that God created males and females with a yearning for love that "burns like a blazing fire, like a vehement flame" that "many waters cannot quench" and "rivers cannot wash away" (Song 8:6-7). For that yearning, that longing, that mad burning eros—if we follow where it *truly leads*—is a "vector of aspiration along which [our] whole existence develops and perfects itself from within" (LR, p. 46).

Where does it truly lead? Eros, properly lived and properly oriented (that's the key!), is our sure ticket to the "ineffable joy experienced by the mystics as 'nuptial union'" (NMI 33). *That's* what we're created for—the bliss of eternal union with God. And *that* is the "true appeal of sexuality," as Pope Benedict wrote. When properly oriented, it puts us on "the path that love opens to God, font of love" (address May 13, 2011). If sin means to "miss the mark," then we have to know what the mark is to know what sin is. And the "mark" is heaven: the eternal bliss of the Marriage of the Lamb. Sin, therefore, is not first and foremost a juridical matter, the breaking of a law. It is first and foremost the breaking of relationship with a loving God; it is a matter of disoriented desire, of seeking satisfaction of our yearning for the Infinite in finite things.[59] Salvation from sin, therefore, always involves redirecting our desire towards that which can truly satisfy—God. As Monsignor Lorenzo Albacete, a beloved professor of mine, expressed it:

> Our hearts desire infinite happiness, infinite satisfaction. Freedom is the capacity for infinity. I am free each time I walk along the path that moves me to infinity . . . If I choose to act in a particular way that separates me from my infinite destiny, I lose something of my freedom and move closer to that abyss of not being free, that is, of "not being able to love anymore." I can be rescued only when the attraction of infinity wins over whatever is attracting me away from it. This is the redemption of my freedom. (GR, p. 113)

We are "attracted away from God" when we have a mistaken notion of who he is. And one of the essential lies we have believed about God is that he's not going to satisfy our desire. "I, the Lord, am your God . . . Open wide your mouth and I will fill it . . . But my people did not heed my voice . . . So I left them in their hardness of heart to follow their own designs" (Ps 81).

We can be saved from sin only when the attraction of who God *really* is (not who we *think* he is based on the Enemy's lies, faulty catechesis, etc.) wins over whatever is attracting us away from him. Indeed, Christ's entire mission is to save us from the lie we believed about God (that he's not our loving Father, that he's not going to satisfy our hunger) and bring us to the eternal Marriage of the Lamb, which Pope Benedict describes as "the supreme moment of satisfaction, in which totality embraces us and we embrace totality." The experience of this satisfaction will be "like plunging into the ocean of infinite love, . . . a plunging ever anew into the vastness of being, in which we are simply overwhelmed with joy." Pope Benedict insists that we "must think along these lines if we want . . . to understand what it is that our faith, our being with Christ, leads us to expect" (SS 12).

The "Touch Point" of Sacred and Secular

Unless existence is cruel, there simply *must* be a banquet that corresponds to the hunger of the human heart. And that's the Gospel message in a nutshell: existence is *not* cruel—there is indeed a banquet that corresponds to our hunger! There is indeed a heavenly bread that offers us the living hope of satisfaction (see Jn 6:35). Bruce Springsteen sings: "Everybody's got a hungry heart," and Mick Jaggar "can't get no sat-tis-fac-tion." Well we Catholics have a song to sing that it seems both of them would be interested in, if we could only find a way to sing it that appealed to their hearts: "You satisfy the hungry heart with gift of finest wheat / Come give to us oh saving Lord the bread of life to eat . . ."

The latter is an example of the "touch point" between the sacred and the secular, and an example of how believers can extend an olive branch and establish a meaningful connection with the popular culture. In the process, we help people see that the Church's vision of human life is not imposed from "without," but wells up from within, from the depths of the human heart and what it really desires. There's obviously a lot wrong with secular culture, but behind every evil there is *always* something good—and we simply must learn how to tease it out. In our zeal to "rid the world of evil," we must be sure to rescue the good that evil distorts. A "theology of affirmation"—seeking out and genuinely affirming even the smallest element of truth wherever it can be found—is a critical element in learning how to "build bridges" with the culture in "an itinerary of friendship," as the Pontifical Council for Culture put it.

Yes, without condoning anything contrary to our faith, we are to develop "an itinerary of friendship" with people like Bruce Springsteen, Mick Jaggar, Lady Gaga, and Hugh Hefner—and the millions of people who emulate them. Like Jesus, we should be willing to sit and eat with them, to enter into dialogue with them, without fearing the fact that we will be misunderstood and even denounced by some for doing so, as was Jesus (see Lk 15:2). It's obviously true that the leaders of popular culture often stand for things antithetical to our faith, but we must resist the temptation to see them only as enemies to be vilified and resisted. They are not the ultimate Enemy with which we are contending: "For we are not contending against flesh and blood, but against the principalities, against the powers, against the rulers of this present darkness" (Eph 6:12). And, just as in the movie *Saving Private Ryan,* we have to be courageous enough to venture behind enemy lines to save those who are captive there. Indeed, loving as Christ loves demands that we do so. But if we are to evangelize the "prostitutes and the sinners," it demands that we be secure enough and mature enough in our own freedom not to be evangelized *by* them, so to speak. If we find ourselves constantly drawn toward the sins they "represent," we'll probably consider *them* the enemy and steer clear of them as if they were modern-day lepers. From this perspective, the secular culture becomes something to be feared and rejected almost entirely. In turn, this fear can become one of the reasons we retreat into our "safe" Catholic bubble, railing against the culture from afar.[60]

In Christ, the sacred comes to the secular both to embrace it and *transform* it. Thus, we mustn't fear the secular culture. Rather, if we are to "carry out the Church's mission of evangelization," as Archbishop Jose Gomez put it, we must become "better students of our culture. We need to understand our culture from the inside out—its values and aspirations, its strengths and weaknesses, its positive and negative aspects. We need always to be on the lookout for new inroads, new avenues and openings for the Gospel, new ways . . . to infuse the spirit of Christianity into our culture" (*You Will Be My Witnesses* 25).

Rather than simply condemning the secular world, with Pope Benedict we must ask: "Where is secularism right? Where can and must the faith adopt the forms and figures of modernity—and where must it offer resistance?" (LW, p. 57). Dismissal of the secular world and the "modern way of thinking" in the name of the Christian faith is *not* the authentic Catholic approach. Quite the contrary: as Benedict XVI insists, we "must strive to integrate the two, in so far as they are compatible with each other." The pope elaborates:

> Being Christian must not become a sort of archaic stratum to which I cling somehow and on which I live to a certain extent *alongside* of modernity. Christianity is itself something living, something modern, which thoroughly shapes and forms all of my modernity—and in this sense actually embraces it. That a major spiritual effort is required here I expressed most recently by founding a "Pontifical Council for Promoting the New Evangelization." It is important for us to try to live Christianity and to think as Christians in such a way that it incorporates what

> is good and right about modernity—and at the same time separates and distinguishes itself from what is [not]. (LW, p. 56)

Why is it so important to Pope Benedict that the new evangelization embrace and incorporate those elements that the modern, secular world gets right? In a word: *connection.* He observes that some formulas conventionally used in expressing the Catholic faith—while "great and true"—"no longer have a place in our overall system of thought and world view." Thus, "they stand in need of new translation and comprehension" (LW, pp. 135-136). Through "a revival of new Catholic initiatives" that come from "the joy of young people," Pope Benedict observes that "Christianity is perhaps acquiring another face and, also, another cultural form." And he optimistically concludes that "Christianity is on the verge of a new dynamic" (LW, p. 59)—a new dynamic, we might add, that is essential if the Gospel is to come "within the horizon of the secular world's understanding" (LW, p. 64).

The Custodians of Beauty

Reading the "signs of the times" and recognizing the particular needs of the Church at this point in history, Popes Paul VI, John Paul II, and Benedict XVI have all recognized that a specific sector of the population is uniquely qualified to offer the Church much needed help in fulfilling her evangelical task: artists.[61]

"We need you," Paul VI said. "We need your collaboration in order to carry out our ministry." For "art consists in grasping treasures from the heavenly realm of the spirit and clothing them in words, colors, forms—making them accessible." Paul VI went so far as to say that without the gift of artists, the Church's ministry "would become faltering and uncertain and a special effort would be needed . . . to make [the Church's ministry] artistic" (address May 7, 1964). John Paul II wrote: "In order to communicate the message entrusted to her by Christ, *the Church needs art*. Art must make perceptible, and as far as possible attractive, the world of the spirit, of the invisible, of God. It must therefore translate into meaningful terms that which is in itself ineffable" (LA 12). And this is not only the role of explicitly religious art. As John Paul II stated:

> Even beyond its typically religious expressions, true art has a close affinity with the world of faith, so that, even in situations where culture and the Church are far apart, art remains a kind of bridge to religious experience. Insofar as it seeks

> the beautiful, . . . art is by its nature a kind of appeal to the mystery. Even when they explore the darkest depths of the soul or the most unsettling aspects of evil, artists give voice in a way to the universal desire for redemption. (LA 10)

Addressing artists as "the custodians of beauty," Pope Benedict XVI observed that authentic beauty "unlocks the yearning of the human heart, the profound desire to know, to love, to go towards the Other, to reach for the Beyond. If we acknowledge that beauty touches us intimately, that it wounds us, that it opens our eyes, then we rediscover the joy of seeing, of being able to grasp the profound meaning of our existence, the Mystery of which we are part" (address November 21, 2009). True art, whether specifically "sacred" or "secular," is by its very nature "religious." Which is to say, it leads us on the "way of beauty," and, if it is faithful to itself, this way leads ultimately to Beauty itself, that is, to God. Benedict elaborates as follows:

> The way of beauty, then, leads us to grasp the Whole in the fragment, the Infinite in the finite, God in the history of humanity. Simone Weil wrote in this regard: "In all that awakens within us the pure and authentic sentiment of beauty, there,

> truly, is the presence of God. There is a kind of incarnation of God in the world, of which beauty is the sign. Beauty is the experimental proof that incarnation is possible. For this reason all art of the first order is, by nature, religious." Hermann Hesse makes the point even more graphically: "Art means: revealing God in everything that exists." (Address November 21, 2009)

And here the pope is not only talking about more refined or "classical art." Along the "way of beauty," the Holy Father maintains that folk art is "no less eloquent and evocative" (address November 21, 2009).

The Way of Beauty

Once again reading the "signs of the times" in order to build bridges with the culture in "an itinerary of friendship," the Pontifical Council for Culture states that "the *Way of Beauty* seems to be a privileged itinerary to get in touch with many of those who face great difficulties in receiving the Church's teachings, particularly regarding morals" (VP II.I). Beauty "creates a fertile terrain to listen and dialogue with men, engaging the whole man—spirit and heart, intelligence and reason, creative capacity and imagination. It is unlikely to result in indifference; it provokes emotions, it puts in movement a dynamism of deep interior transformation" (VP II.3).

In this way, "the simple experience of the marvel-arousing meeting with beauty, the *via pulchritudinis* [the way of beauty] can open the pathway for the search for God." It "disposes the heart and spirit to meet Christ, who is the Beauty of Holiness Incarnate . . . It invites contemporary Augustines, unquenchable seekers of love, truth and beauty, to see through perceptible beauty to eternal Beauty, and with fervor discover Holy God, the author of all beauty." (VP II.I) Ah!—contemporary Augustines! These are the men and women of today who, in seeking the satisfaction and beauty they crave, have exhausted the pleasures of created things—pleasures they had idolized—and are now open to *the One* who created all such pleasures in order to lead us to his own glory and bliss. St. Augustine describes the dramatic reorientation of his yearning from created beauty to Uncreated Beauty in this famous passage from his *Confessions*:

> Late have I loved you, O Beauty ever ancient, ever new, late have I loved you! You were within me, but I was outside, and it was there that I searched for you. In my unloveliness I plunged into the lovely things which you created. You were with

> me, but I was not with you. Created things kept me from you; yet if they had not been in you they would not have been at all. You called, you shouted, and you broke through my deafness. You flashed, you shone, and you dispelled my blindness. You breathed your fragrance on me; I drew in breath and now I pant for you. I have tasted you, now I hunger and thirst for more. You touched me, and I burned for your peace. (Bk 10, chap 26, 27.37)

Those who know something of this experience—this inhaling of the divine fragrance, this panting, this hunger, this thirst for more and more of the divine sweetness, this interior *burning*—cannot *not* invite others along this *Way of Beauty* . . . this way that, if we stay the course "through many dangers, toils, and snares," eventually "passes over" from "the visible to the invisible, from the sign to the thing signified" (CCC 1075).

True Beauty has the ability to snap us out of our lukewarmness and gives us "wings" to make this pass-over. An "essential function of genuine beauty," as Pope Benedict wrote, "is that it gives man a healthy 'shock,' it draws him out of himself, wrenches him away from . . . being content with the humdrum—it even makes him suffer, piercing him like a dart, but in so doing it 'reawakens' him, opening afresh the eyes of his heart and mind, giving him wings, carrying him aloft" (address, November 21, 2009).[62]

We might say that John Paul II's TOB is the invitation *par excellence* to venture along the *Way of Beauty*. It is an invitation not to fear the "healthy shock" that the beauty of the human body causes in us. But here, in a particularly clear way, we must distinguish the true beauty of the human body from its many alluring counterfeits. We must distinguish the "healthy shock" of the beauty of the body from the all too prevalent "unhealthy shock" caused by a pornographic portrayal (or, rather, *be*trayal) of the human body.

The Link of Beauty and Truth

As the Pontifical Council for Culture observes, "the *Way of Beauty* is not exempt from ambiguity, deviations, errors, detours, etc." For "beauty is only authentic in its link with truth" (VP II.I). Indeed, the two—truth and beauty—stand or fall together. Truth without beauty is no longer true to itself, and beauty without truth ushers in a great ugliness. In effect, we will *scorn* truth without beauty and we will *porn* beauty without truth. Allow me to explain.

When the Church's teaching is presented without beauty—in a dry, cold, mechanical, doctrinaire way, for example—the heart rarely (if ever) responds, even if what's being presented is true. Worse still, when the Church's teaching is set to an "ugly tune," so to speak—for example, when our presentation of truth is tinged with self-righteousness, condemnation, accusation, or judgmentalism—the truth can even come across as an affront to our hearts. And when this happens, our hearts revolt—with good reason: we're made for beauty. That's what I mean by saying we scorn truth without beauty. Conversely, when we seek beauty as an end in itself, cutting it off from truth—the truth of God and the truth of the human person made in God's image—we "porn" it. By this I mean we reduce beauty to the merely physical level and fixate ourselves on it for the sake of a selfish, base gratification of our bodily senses, cut off from transcendental truth. When this happens, it is

> the captivating flowers of evil [that] fascinate: "Are you from the highest heaven or out of the abyss, O beauty?" pondered Baudelaire. And Dimitri Karamazov confided to his

> brother Aliocha: "Beauty is a terrible thing. It is the struggle between God and Satan, the battleground, my heart." If beauty is the image of the creator God, it is also the child of Adam and Eve and so in turn marked by sin. The human person risks falling into the trap of beauty taken for itself—the icon become idol, the means that swallow the end . . . due to an inadequate formation in the senses and the lack of a proper education regarding beauty. (VP II.2)

Traveling the *Way of Beauty*, therefore, implies an education in authentic beauty. It necessitates learning the art of discernment, which is the ability to distinguish the wheat from the weeds. Since these inevitably grow together, one cannot conclude that the wheat is "in the Church" (the sacred realm) and the weeds are "in the culture" (the secular realm). There are plenty of weeds to be found within the Church, just as there is plenty of wheat to be found in the culture. We must be clear on both and call both out.

Traveling the *Way of Beauty* also means insisting that the truth be presented in all its radiant splendor, in a way that truly captivates the heart. If we are to evangelize the modern world, we *must* set the Church's teaching to the "right music." We must present the truth in such a way that it "sings." As a priest once shared with me, "A truth that does not sing is a truth betrayed." When we come into contact with the Mystery—not merely as an intellectual idea, but as the experience of a love that "sears through us like a flame" (SS 47)—truth becomes song. Cardinal Ratzinger put it this way: "When man comes into contact with God, mere speech is not enough. Areas of his existence are awakened that spontaneously turn into song" (SL, p. 136).

Entering the Song

The Bible's opening chapters culminate in the marriage of Adam and Eve. The Bible's final chapters culminate in the marriage of Christ and the Church. And right in the middle of the Bible we find an unabashed celebration of erotic love that lays claim to the title: "greatest song ever written"—the Song of Songs. According to Pope Benedict XVI, this erotic love poetry expresses "the essence of biblical faith" (DC 10). As I wrote in my book *Heaven's Song*:

> Why is the Song of Songs the favorite biblical book of the mystics? Why have the saints written

more commentaries on this seemingly obscure and wildly erotic love poetry than on any other book in the Bible? . . . What do they know that most Christians seem not to? If this is "heaven's song" transposed into a human key, then, as the saints and mystics know, the Song of Songs is the authentic soundtrack of Christianity.

The Church has an incredibly joyful song to sing. It's the song of the Bride rejoicing in total surrender to the love of her Bridegroom. "It is the utter depth of love that produces [her] singing," Pope Benedict tells us. Then he quotes St. Augustine: "'*Cantare amantis est*' . . . singing is a lover's thing." The Church's love song, in fact, is "the new tongue that comes from the Holy Spirit." In this heavenly song, says Benedict, the Church experiences "an inebriation surpassing all the possibilities of mere rationality" (SL, pp. 140, 142). In other words, we can't enter the joy—the "inebriation"—of the Church's love song merely with our minds, merely with an intellectual, rational grasp of theological ideas, however "correct" those ideas might be. Singing comes from a different "place" within the human being: from the depths of the heart. (HS, p. 24)

In short, we must not be afraid to *enter the love Song* God is singing to us and learn how to *sing back*. "*Cantare amantis est*"—singing is a lover's thing. Indeed, I believe that every love song ever written (and how many have been written!) is an attempt, however broken, to do just this—to enter the Song of Songs. For even misdirected eros is a sign of the kind of beings we are: lovers created for everlasting Love—which is just another way of saying creatures with the capacity and yearning for God. All we need do is turn on the radio and—if we listen—we will hear the cry of the human heart for love, which is to say, we will hear the cry of the human heart for Christ, even from those whom we might be tempted to consider "far from him."

Reaching the "Twisted Mystics"

Inasmuch as a culture's songs provide a window into its soul, the rise of rock music in the 1950s and '60s is very telling. If the Song of Songs is the "soundtrack" of Christianity, "rock and roll" music could be described as the "soundtrack" of the sexual revolution.[63] And if the Song of Songs gives voice to the deepest yearnings and sentiments of the mystics, I'd say rock music gives voice to the deepest yearnings and sentiments of those I call the "twisted mystics." The Song of Songs expresses properly directed eros. Rock and roll often expresses misdirected eros. But again, even misdirected eros shows us the kind of beings we are: creatures of desire who long for God. "Untwist" the distortions of the "twisted mystics," and what do we find? We glimpse something of the mysticism of the Song of Songs, and we come to see that those men and women behind the music are so many "contemporary Augustines" who need help in seeing what it is they're really looking for. They don't need our condemnation. They need our encouragement! *They're onto something.*

Just as the Babylonians yearned for the Israelites to sing to them the songs of Zion (see Ps 137), so, too, do the "twisted mystics" yearn for us to sing to them the Song of Songs. And we can find a meaningful connection with them by recognizing the elements of truth already present in what they're singing about. Where reality has been "twisted" in their songs, perhaps we can help "untwist" it, showing them that Christ has been hidden in their heart's music all along. As I have learned over the years, doing so can become a powerful catechetical tool in sharing the Gospel.[64] John Paul II, himself, took this approach with the music of Bob Dylan after the famous singer performed at the 1997 Eucharistic Congress in Bologna. Quoting from Dylan's Song "Blowin' in the

Wind," John Paul asked, "'How many roads must a man walk before he becomes a man'? I answer you, One! There is only one road for man and it is Christ." And what is the answer "blowing in the wind"? "The breath and voice of the Spirit," John Paul insisted, "a voice that calls and says, 'Come'" (address, September 17, 1997).[65]

Using popular music as a teaching tool in this way is an example of how we can help people see and experience the world "sacramentally." The more we enter this sacramental vision, the more "we realize that God is everywhere," as Caryll Houselander says, "and everything reminds us of him." Even a banal pop song we hear on the radio can now be "informed with a totally different meaning." She continues: "Life as we have made it is indeed as cheap and tawdry as any popular song, but just because we now must be reminded of the beloved [God] by every line of it and every note of it, it has become pure music and exquisite poetry for us." This is what happens, says Houselander, when our desire for God takes hold of us: life becomes "like a popular song which haunts us" (RG, p. 174). And we come to realize that all of creation is singing this divine love song. We realize that the hills are indeed "alive, with the sound of music," with a "folk song" that proclaims the mystery of the Incarnation.

Yes, the "song of the Incarnation is a folk song," Houselander tells us. "In it is all the primal love and joy and sorrow of all the world. It explains and simplifies all human lives in all times . . . It is the song of the lover standing at the door. It is the song of the bridegroom singing to the bride" (RG, pp. 87-88). And we must learn how to sing back. It's called *holiness.* For "holiness is measured according to the 'great mystery' in which the Bride responds with the gift of love to the gift of the Bridegroom" (CCC 773). And it is this "song of the Bride"—Mary's song—that above all else reveals the *Way of Beauty* that evangelizes the world.

Mary Reveals the Way of Beauty

In the upper right-hand corner of John Paul II's original, handwritten TOB manuscript is the date he started writing it: December 8, 1974—feast of Mary's Immaculate Conception. And just above that date, in an adaptation of a key verse from the Song of Songs (see Song 4:7), we see to whom John Paul II dedicated his masterwork: "*tota pulchra es Maria*" ("you are all beautiful, Mary"). And so, at the close of these reflections, we turn to Mary. For she "goes before us all in the holiness that is the Church's mystery as 'the bride without spot or wrinkle' "

(CCC 773). She, as "the most perfect illustration of the work of beauty" (VP III.3), reveals the *Way of Beauty.*

During the first canonization ceremony of his pontificate, Benedict XVI expressed that "the saint is the one who is so fascinated by the beauty of God and by his perfect truth that he is progressively transformed by it" (address October 23, 2005). Beauty itself took on flesh in the womb of Mary, and "gave himself up" for us so that we, seized by divine Beauty, might be made all beautiful (see Eph 5:25-27). Unfortunately, few people perceive Christianity as an invitation to be "seized by Beauty," or to be "made beautiful by Beauty." Instead, as the Pontifical Council for Culture laments, "many people perceive Christianity as a submission to commandments made up of prohibitions and limits applied to personal liberty" (VP III.3).

When we reduce holiness to a "prim and proper" following of an ethical code, we have sapped Christianity of its radiant beauty and evangelical appeal, effectively replacing the *burning fire* that Christ came to ignite in the human heart with a cold life of "duty." The first words of Christ recorded in the Gospel of John bring us to the heart of the matter. They are not a call to "get our acts together" and conform our behavior to a list of rules.

Rather, John *the Evangelist* begins Christ's "liturgy of the word" with a question that resounds in every human heart throughout the ages: "*What are you looking for?*" (Jn 1:38).

In short, Christianity is a religion of desire, a religion that proclaims blessed "those who hunger and thirst." Pope Benedict observes that when St. Augustine describes man as a creature of desire, driven towards some unknown fulfillment, he "is describing man's essential situation" in a "permanently valid way" (SS 12). "Our life is a gymnasium of desire," says Augustine. "When we say 'God,' what do we wish to express? This word is all that we yearn for" (*Homily on First Letter of John*). "Religion," therefore, as Monsignor Albacete once put it, "is either the reasonable quest for the satisfaction of all the original desires of the heart, or it is a dangerous, divisive, harmful waste of time" (GR, p. 154).

Olivier Clement, an Orthodox author and professor of Eastern spirituality, reflects on the vast difference of conceiving of Christianity as a "keeping of the law" vs. that of a "longing for the Infinite." We have leaned so heavily on our own supposed ability to "please God" by following the rules that, for "a moment we must lose our balance, must see in a flash of clarity . . . the ripping apart of our protective covering of happiness or moral virtue."

If we allow ourselves to be stripped in this way, it will draw out of us "a cry of trust and love *de profundis,* from the depths of the heart." And it will enable us to rediscover "our own finiteness, and at the same time our longing for the infinite, that we are not self-sufficient, that we have not the source of joy within ourselves." He elaborates:

> In the Gospel the very root of sin is the pretense that we can save ourselves by our own effort . . . The publicans and harlots enter the Kingdom before the just because they are well aware that they cannot save themselves; knowing the wretchedness of their condition, they are open to the Love that has come within their reach. So [their turning to Christ] is not only the result of guilty feelings. It is the consciousness of a desire that cannot be satisfied, the inner emptiness crying out to be filled with it knows not what. "The hearts of human beings," says Nicolas Cabasilas, "were made great enough to contain God himself." If they do not contain the Uncreated they will turn their desire toward created objects, and then only nothingness can spring forth, for every person is a gaping space waiting to be filled with God. (As cited in *Magnificat,* April 2009, p. 61)

And this brings us back to Mary. As a witness to the path that alone leads to Life, Mary is the one who opened that "gaping space" within her "to be filled with God" and thus literally "contained the Uncreated." Receiving a "bread from heaven" beyond her wildest imaginings, she exclaims: "He has filled the hungry with good things" (Lk 1:53). In this way, Mary's witness saves us from a "false eternity," to use an expression of Benedict XVI's. "You see, man strives for eternal joy; he would like pleasure in the extreme, would like what is eternal. But when there is no God . . . he himself must now create something that is fictitious, a false eternity" (LW, p. 61).

Oh! How tragic that we have believed the lie that God does not want to grant the desires of our hearts! Our desire for "eternal joy," for "pleasure in the extreme" is not bad. That's not the problem; God created us that way. He put that desire in our hearts so that we, like a bride, might open our longing to "the gift" of the eternal Bridegroom. The tragedy—where we have sinned—is that we have doubted "the gift," as John Paul II put it (see TOB 26:4). And if we believe that God is not going to *grant* us the heaven we desire, we will attempt to satisfy our desire for "pleasure in the extreme" on our own. If heaven is not real, then we will probably set our sights on the next best thing—that primary *icon* of heaven found here in the created world: sex. But alas, this "false heaven" ends up creating a living hell. Indeed, hell is the heaven *we* create because we don't believe in (or aren't willing to wait for) the heaven God wants to give us. We want heaven ("pleasure in the extreme") on our own terms. Welcome to the pornographic "culture of death" in which the primary *icon* has become our primary *idol.*

The unbridled pursuit of pleasure is "a sign of the times," Pope Benedict tells us, "that should be an urgent challenge to us, especially as Christians." How should Christians respond to this urgent challenge? "We have to show—and also live this accordingly—that the eternity man needs can come only from God . . . so that a genuine coin can stand up against the false coin—and in this way the cycle of evil can be broken and stopped" (LW, p. 61). The cycle of evil *has* been broken and stopped in Mary, because she was the first to receive the fullness of redemption in Christ. Full of grace, she was the first to resist the seduction of the "false coin" and open her longing for infinite riches to the "genuine coin"—Jesus Christ.

"What are you looking for?" Christ asks. In the prelude to his discourse on "the Bread of Life," he lovingly assures us: *"Amen, amen, I say to you, you are looking for me . . ."* (Jn 6:26). If the evil of our pornographic culture is to be stopped, we mustn't condemn the body and sex, nor seek to snuff out the fire of eros that lies at the core of our humanity. Rather, we must rediscover the true meaning of the body and sex as a sign of the "great mystery" of Christ's love for the Church, redirecting eros towards its true object. As Father Cantalamessa put it, "the primary object of our eros, of our search, desire, attraction, passion must be Christ" (TF 4). This is the way evil is stopped: "we must become a longing for God," says Pope Benedict. In other words, we must learn how to *pray.* For "prayer, properly understood, is nothing but becoming a longing for God" (MCS, p. 15).

As the first of the Lord's disciples, Mary, once again, is our primary witness and model. She is "the open vessel of longing, in which life becomes prayer and prayer becomes life" (MCS, p. 15). She is the open vessel of longing who trusted in "the gift," and who received "the gift"—conceiving the Infinite *in her flesh.* Mary shows us that by opening our longing to God, eros becomes a force for our salvation rather than our destruction. In fact, it becomes the means by which Christ enters the world and *sets us on Fire.* So, then, let us open our eros to this divine Fire. Let us open our eros to *Eros.* It's in this way that we participate in the "great mystery" that lies at the heart of the Gospel and reclaim the body for the new evangelization.

Mary, set ablaze with God's Eros, pray for us that we would not fear the Fire that Christ, your Son, came to cast upon the earth. Teach us how to burn . . . Amen.

ACKNOWLEDGMENTS

Although I didn't begin writing this book until after the completion of an extended sabbatical in 2010, this work is a fruit of that sabbatical. So I would first like to thank all those men and women (too numerous to mention by name) who made that extended and necessary time of prayer and reflection possible. I would also like to thank my critics. Your challenges have sharpened me, refined me, and encouraged me to dig even deeper into the thought and wisdom of John Paul II.

The following men and women read various drafts of my manuscript and offered helpful feedback. Without their help this book would not have taken its current shape. My deep gratitude goes to Wendy West, Matt Pinto, Steve Motyl, Mark Wassmer, Bonnie West, Jennifer Simmons, Mike Mangione, Jen Messing, David Kang, Jason Clark, Nathan West, Chris Cope, Mike Flickinger, Soren West, Jay Wonacott, Christopher Paul, Jim Otto, William May, Michael Waldstein, Lorenzo Albacete, Janet Smith, Karen Goodwin, Greg Weidman, Bill Donaghy, Helen Scieszka, and John Crosby.

Appendices

Appendix I

Let the Marriage Bed Be Undefiled

Let marriage be held in honor among all, and let the marriage bed be undefiled. (Heb 13: 4)

When I started teaching marriage preparation and enrichment courses in the mid-late nineties, I would give couples the opportunity to ask questions anonymously by putting them to paper and placing them in a box. One hundred and fifteen of the most commonly asked questions became the basis of my book *Good News about Sex and Marriage: Answers to Your Honest Questions about Catholic Teaching.* Because of a statement in the first edition of that book that has been taken out of context, some believe (wrongly) that I endorse "sodomy" in marriage.

One would wish never to have to address such unseemly topics. Alas, because of the gravity of the matter, it demands some attention, if only in an appendix.[66]

The Objective Moral Principle

Many married couples in the Church today are looking for sound moral guidance on questions of appropriate foreplay to sexual intercourse. As I wrote in *Good News about Sex and Marriage*, "You're not going to find an official Magisterial statement addressing [specific issues of foreplay] directly. But the principles we've . . . outlined in this book enable us to draw sound conclusions" (GNSM, p. 92). The basic moral principle I outline is based on the long-held position of orthodox moral theologians about the *telos* or *end* of the sexual act (more specifically, the *telos* or *end* of the man's ejaculation of seed). It is well expressed by Lawler, Boyle, and May in their book *Catholic Sexual Ethics*. They write that the Church's teaching that one's sexual acts must remain "open to life"

> applies not only to the use of contraceptive devices but also to any acts done with the intention of preventing a complete genital act between spouses from being a potentially life-giving act. Thus, mutual masturbation, oral and anal sex, and similar acts in which orgasms are sought apart from natural intercourse, are gravely wrong. (CSE, p. 164)

"Complete" genital acts refer to genital stimulation to the point of sexual climax. Because of the inherent link between a man's sexual climax, his giving of his seed, and procreation, the only proper context for his ejaculation is in the natural act of vaginal intercourse.[67] But this

> does not imply that mutual genital stimulation other than intercourse is forbidden for spouses as part of the preliminaries to marital intercourse. Marriage is a mutual commitment in which each side ceases to be autonomous, in various ways and also sexually: the sexual liberty in agreement together is great; here, so long as they are not immoderate so as to become slaves of sensuality, nothing is shameful, if the complete acts—the ones involving ejaculation of the man's seed—that they engage in are real and true marriage acts [i.e., ejaculation must take place in vaginal intercourse]. But the qualification in this statement is important. The activities of the spouses must be moderate, and the danger of becoming "slaves of sensuality" is real. (CSE, p. 164)

So, again—according to the broad consensus of orthodox moral theologians—the one sure, objective criteria for evaluating the sexual behavior of spouses is that their physical intimacies must culminate in the natural act of marital intercourse, with the husband ejaculating *only* in his wife's vagina. This is the natural end (*telos*) of ejaculation. Logical moralists recognize (and one must base his conclusions here on logic, not emotion, however strong or understandable such emotion may be) that this objective norm does not, in itself, exclude (non-ejaculatory) foreplay involving what the Dominican Fr. Benoit Merkelbach tactfully described as "the undue vessel."

In his authoritative moral manual of 1936, Merkelbach wrote: "To begin union in the undue vessel, e.g., the backward vessel . . . with the intention of consummating it in the vagina, and again to touch the backward vessel with the genitals . . . is not a mortal sin, as long as the pouring out of semen is prevented and the sodomitic emotion is excluded . . . Indeed, when they are sought as the only means and preparation for the due act and a sufficient reason is present, e.g., because someone cannot be aroused in another way, then they are not a sin" (QD, p. 110).

To cite another example, Fr. Heribert Jone wrote in his highly regarded 1956 book *Moral Theology*: "Excluding the sodomitic intention [that is, the intention to ejaculate] it is neither sodomy nor a grave sin if intercourse is begun in a rectal manner with the intention of consummating it naturally" (section 757). The fact that this book was reprinted by TAN in 1993—a publisher that prides itself in its fidelity to the Catholic Tradition—certainly speaks to the orthodoxy of this teaching. Indeed, in the preface to Jone's book we read: "The fact that this book went through 18 editions in German, as well as in its English translation, and was translated also into seven other languages is ample testimony that it was accepted universally throughout the Catholic Church as authoritative and reliable."

Beyond the "Objective Principle"

One might think I am citing the above theologians because I share their rather benign evaluation of such behavior. I do not. If one cannot condemn foreplay in the "undue vessel" based on the objective principle that necessitates ejaculation in the "due vessel," then one can—and, in my firm opinion, *should*—condemn (or, at a minimum, *strongly, in no uncertain terms* discourage) such behavior based on many other factors.

Objective principles or "legal norms" are not enough in evaluating human behavior. As John Paul II observed, "discernment of good and evil inscribed in human conscience can turn out to be deeper and more correct than the content of a legal norm" (TOB 35:5). Beyond the "legal norm" of ensuring that ejaculation takes place during the act of natural intercourse, we must ask several other questions to evaluate the morality of foreplay involving the "undue vessel" (as with questions of all types of foreplay). For example: What is the intention of spouses in such behavior? What's going on in their hearts? Why would someone do this? What desire does such behavior purport to satisfy? Is it a good desire? All of these questions *must* be taken into account.

And here my teaching is closer to that of St. Alphonsus Liguori than to that of Jone and Merkelbach. Liguori condemns such behavior not because it contradicts the inherent orientation of ejaculation. Rather, Liguori believes such behavior cannot happen "without sodomitic emotion" (TM 6.469). In other words, he believes spouses who engage in this behavior demonstrate a serious distortion in their emotional dispositions, as do I.[68]

In the first edition of *Good News about Sex and Marriage*, based on the objective principle that a "husband should never intentionally ejaculate anywhere but his wife's vagina," I repeated the teaching of Merkelbach and Jone that there is "nothing *inherently* wrong with anal penetration as foreplay to normal intercourse" (GNSM, first edition, p. 93). This is the statement that various authors latched on to, reporting that I promote "sodomy" in marriage. What wasn't reported is the fact that I immediately followed this statement with three paragraphs of strong, frank reasons why such behavior could not and should not be condoned. In the revised edition of my book, I detailed with even stronger language why, despite any appeal to the objective principle, "it is very difficult to justify anal penetration as a loving act of foreplay to the marital embrace." It's my firm belief that such behavior stems "much more from the disorder of lust than from a genuine desire to symbolize and renew the marriage commitment" (GNSM, p. 94).

John Kippley, founder of the Couple to Couple League, offers another example of how an orthodox teacher of the faith handled this matter. He wrote that "the traditional moral question has to do with completed . . . anal sex in which either male or female orgasm occurs apart from completed genital-genital relations. Traditional Catholic theology has called [such completed acts of foreplay] perversities." However, Kippley observed that "vaginal intercourse immediately after anal penetration (incomplete foreplay) would be so unsanitary that it is difficult to imagine any possibly moral use of anal copulation" (SMC, p. 47).

This is all one can do if he is to be faithful to the theological consensus: acknowledge that the behavior in question does not in itself violate the objective principle, but find other grounds for refusing to condone it. If some moralists wish to offer an absolute condemnation of such acts of foreplay, they must acknowledge the fact that they would be contradicting the long-held theological consensus and provide well-reasoned explanations for doing so. If in the future, the Magisterium should contradict that consensus and offer a simple and objective condemnation of such behavior, I would embrace it without hesitation. However, I do not have authority of my own to contradict that consensus.

Appendix II

BAPTISM IS A NUPTIAL MYSTERY

Baptism, the entry into the People of God, is a nuptial mystery. [It] is a bath of water in which the "imperishable seed" of the Word of God produces its life-giving effect.

—Catechism of the Catholic Church (1617 and 1228)

We have learned in this work that all of the Church's sacraments find their "prototype" in some way in the sacrament of marriage, in the "great mystery" by which a man and woman join the whole of their lives together so intimately as to be "one flesh." In what follows, we will explore a particularly vivid example of nuptial symbolism in the liturgical ritual of the Church, that of the blessing of the baptismal waters during the Easter Vigil.

I first learned of the nuptial significance of this ritual from a book published by Ignatius Press called *Sex and Sacredness.* Therein, the British essayist Christopher Derrick very creatively guides the reader through a reflection on the masculine and feminine symbols of this rite and their "sacred marriage" (see SAS, pp. 67-73). I never imagined that sharing this vision with a Catholic audience would cause such a stir. However, as Derrick observed, there are, indeed, "a number of respects in which the Church can be a good deal more shocking than some kinds of Catholic piety would wish it to be" (SAS, p. 72).

In the first part of what follows, we'll carefully unfold the nuptial meaning of Baptism as a sacrament in which Christ and the Church—the Bridegroom and the Bride—bring forth children unto eternal life through their mystical union. We'll conclude by reflecting on the power of the liturgy to open our eyes to the holiness and beauty of this "great mystery."

Liturgy as a "Spousal Mystery"

Drawing deeply from the theological tradition, John Paul II's TOB presents a "spousal theology" to us—which is not just a *theological* way of viewing spouses, but also a *spousal* way of viewing theology. In turn, this leads to a *liturgical* way of viewing spouses and a *spousal* way of viewing the liturgy. All of this comes to light through what John Paul II calls "the prophetic 'language of the body'" (see TOB 104).

The body has a "prophetic language" inasmuch as it is meant to proclaim the "great mystery" of Christ and his eternal love for the Church. For spouses, this happens throughout married life as they express their faithful commitment to each other through the "sincere gift of self"—in good times and bad, sickness and health, etc. But this "language of gift" finds its consummate expression in the marital embrace. John Paul II put it this way: "All married life is a gift, but this becomes most evident when the spouses, in giving themselves to each other in love, bring about that encounter which makes them 'one flesh'" (LF 12). "In this way, through the 'language of the body,' man and woman encounter the great '*mysterium*' in order to transfer the light of this mystery . . . into the 'language of the body' . . . On this road, conjugal life in some sense becomes liturgy" (TOB 117b:6).

Before I express the next idea, we would do well to ponder for a moment how stunningly beautiful the vision is which John Paul II lays before us (and for more than a moment!—indeed we should take these glorious truths with us into times of extended prayer, allowing them more and more to heal and cleanse us of any diseased ideas and images of our bodies and our sexuality). In John Paul II's teaching on the "liturgical" reality of conjugal life, we catch a glimpse of the glory and profundity of sexual love in the Church's authentic vision of it. Here, as John Paul II says, we should be "full of veneration for *the essential values of conjugal union* . . . of the conjugal act." For it "bears in itself the sign of the divine mystery of creation and redemption" (TOB 131:5). The conjugal act itself, John Paul tells us, as the consummate expression of the sacrament of marriage, is meant to be an expression and participation in the "life of the Holy Spirit" (see TOB 101:6), that is, in the very life of the Holy Trinity. As an aside, we might ask, from this perspective: *Who takes human sexuality more seriously—a culture that treats sexual activity as base entertainment and expresses it as casually as a handshake, or a Church that views it as a "sacramental" and "liturgical" reality that, as Pope Benedict XVI tells us, "tends to rise 'in ecstasy' towards the Divine"* (DC 5)?

The language of marital love is so holy, so sacred precisely because it draws its depth and meaning from the language of the liturgy—that is, from the "great mystery" of Christ's love for the Church. Furthermore, because the spousal analogy moves in two directions, "one also sees the way in which *the language and ritual* of the liturgy *are modeled after the 'language of the body'*" (TOB 117:6)—which is to say, the Church's liturgy is modeled after the "great mystery" of spousal love and union.[69] Liturgy is the very manner by which the Church, as the Bride of Christ, opens herself to receive and reciprocate the gift of her Bridegroom's love. For when the Church prays, the future Pope Benedict observed, she "tries to approach the Lord and thus seeks to enter into nuptial union with him" (SL, p. 197).

Here we see very clearly that the spousal mystery is not only present in certain aspects of the Church's life, or tucked away in a corner. As the *Catechism* observes, "The entire Christian life bears the mark of the spousal love of Christ and the Church.[70] Already Baptism, the entry into the People of God, is a nuptial mystery; it is so to speak the nuptial bath which precedes the wedding feast, the Eucharist" (CCC 1617).

To say Baptism is a "nuptial mystery" is to recognize, as John Paul II observes, that "Baptism draws its essential significance and sacramental strength from the Redeemer's spousal love" (TOB 99:1)—a love that, being truly "spousal," is both "unitive" and "life-giving" (see TOB 97:4). The idea of Baptism as a "nuptial bath" comes from Ephesians 5:25-26—"Christ loved the Church and gave himself up for her, that he might sanctify her, having cleansed her by the washing of water accompanied by the word." This "washing," John Paul tells us, is "*the expression of spousal love.*" It "makes the Church the Bride of Christ" (TOB 91:7). In turn, when Christ's spousal love is poured out in the sacrament of Baptism, his Church-Bride "brings forth sons, who are conceived by the Holy Spirit and born of God, to a new and immortal life" (CCC 507).

This is a *virginal* birth, of course, by grace. The offspring of the New Adam and the New Eve are born not of the flesh, not of a husband's physical seed, nor of a physical (genital) union, "but of God" (Jn 1:13). Nonetheless, based on all we learned in chapter five, there is a certain analogy between the two orders (nature and grace). Since grace builds on nature, the natural way of conception and birth serves in some way as the model, the "prototype" of supernatural conception and birth. "How did the old humanity begin?" asks Fulton Sheen. "With the nuptials. How will the new humanity begin? With the nuptials . . . There is here the birth of the Church" (FS, p. 60). And this fruitfulness, as we explained in chapter five, while certainly virginal "is by no means asexual" (NM, p. 270).

Signs of the Bridegroom and of the Bride in the Rite of Baptism

"By following the gestures and words" of the celebration of Baptism "with attentive participation," the *Catechism* says that "the faithful are initiated into the riches this sacrament signifies" (CCC 1234). Among other things, as we've been learning, Baptism signifies the "new birth" of a Christian via the virginal (but not asexual) nuptials of Christ and the Church. And this "new birth in the Holy Spirit" is "signified by the perceptible elements of the sacramental rite" (CCC 1262). Where? How? Let's take a look by "following the gestures and words of this celebration" attentively, as the *Catechism* suggests. In other words, let us gently lift a corner of the veil, to see if we can notice signs of the Bridegroom and of the Bride, of their mystical union—"clothed" as it is in the "figure and form" of natural union—and of the power of their union to generate "new life in the Spirit."

Inscribed in the baptistry of the Pope's Cathedral in Rome (the Archbasilica of St. John Lateran), we read: "At this font, the Church, our mother, gives birth from her virginal womb to the children she conceived by the power of the Holy Spirit." If the baptismal font is a liturgical sign of the Church's "womb," as theological tradition has long held,[71] it should not surprise us to see in the liturgical rite some sign of the Bridegroom's presence and life-giving gift as well. And this is precisely the significance (the "sign value") of the priest and the action he performs in this rite. As the sacramental presence of Christ the Bridegroom, during the rite of Baptism at the Easter Vigil, the priest submerges the Christ candle into the font (once or three times) and prays for the Spirit to descend upon the water "so that those who will be baptized in it may be 'born of water and the Spirit' " (CCC 1238).

"The meaning is profound," writes Monsignor Nicola Bux.[72] We can recognize in the symbolism of the ritual that "the priest is the fertilizing organ of the ecclesial womb . . . Truly in the person of Christ Head he engenders children that, as father, he fortifies with the chrism and nourishes with the Eucharist. Also," Bux concludes, "by reason of the marital functions to the Church Bride, the priest must be a man. All the mystical meaning of Easter is manifested in the priestly identity, coming to fullness, the pleroma, as the East says."[73]

The "new birth in the Holy Spirit" which is "signified by the perceptible elements of the sacramental rite" (CCC 1262) reveals Baptism to be a "nuptial mystery" (CCC

1617) "in which the 'imperishable seed' of the Word of God produces its life-giving effect" (CCC 1228). The "imperishable seed" is given by Christ as Bridegroom and received by the Church as Bride. And through these glorious, virginal nuptials the Church "brings forth sons . . . to a new and immortal life" (CCC 507).[74]

Suspicion Towards the Body?

While the symbolism of "masculine generativity" in the priest and the symbolism of "feminine generativity" in the baptismal font offers us a beautiful way of entering into the "nuptial mystery" of Baptism, the nuptial reading is not the only valid reading of this rite. A preference for a different reading is fine. However, there are some authors, including some high-ranking liturgists, who not only prefer a different reading, but denounce the nuptial reading. Some even imply that those who recognize an analogy to spousal union in the ritual must be perverse, and to teach such a reading of the ritual is tantamount to placing people in an occasion of sin. But does this idea not flow from a "hermeneutic of suspicion"—from an interpretation of man that holds him bound to his lustful distortions without the possibility of liberation? Such a view of man—the belief that everything to do with sex must be perverse—as Karol Wojtyla wrote, "smacks of Manichaeism" (LR, p. 188).

We must certainly be sensitive in presenting the nuptial imagery of this rite, especially in today's cultural climate (I acknowledge that my early work lacked this at times). However, if our primary reaction to such imagery is discomfort or fear, perhaps the solution is not to reject the imagery. Perhaps the solution is to examine whether our own ideas about the body and sexuality may be preventing us from recognizing the holiness and beauty of the imagery. The journey of inner purification is a very long and very difficult one. It's much easier to eschew the body and sexuality than it is to face the disorders in our hearts that cause us to do so. But, as stated earlier, we must be very careful here. For eschewing the body in this way would signify a certain acceptance of the Manichaean mentality. It would not constitute "a real and deep victory" over the evil in our hearts (see TOB 45:4). In fact, such an approach "might—and may always be—a loophole to avoid the requirements set in the Gospel" (TOB 44:6), the requirements of "a full purification" (TOB 116:3).

Yet again we are back to that pivotal question: is it possible for man to overcome the domination of concupiscence? Is it possible for man to see and experience the sexual sphere as an encounter with and revelation of "the holy"? If we need to beware of slipping into "Freudian thought" in our evaluation of sexuality—as various Christian authors rightly caution—then I will offer the same caution and humbly point out that that is precisely what's happening when we bind man to his lusts.

The Meaning of Life Is at Stake in the Way We "See"

John Paul II describes Freud as a "master of suspicion" precisely because he binds man to the concupiscence of the flesh, imagining that man's lustful "libido" is all there is when it comes to sexual matters (see TOB 46:1-2).[75] But, as John Paul insists, Christ's teaching "does not allow us to stop here. Although Christ's words in Matthew 5:27-28 [about committing adultery in the 'heart'] show the whole reality of desire and concupiscence, they do not allow us to turn such concupiscence into the absolute principle of anthropology and ethics" (TOB 46:2).

In other words, who we are as human beings (anthropology) and how we should conduct ourselves (ethics) is not determined solely, or even primarily, by the fact that we are fallen, sinful creatures. Of course that must be taken into account, but we are *more* than that. Much more! As John Paul II declared in his homily at

World Youth Day in 2002, "We are not the sum of our weaknesses and failures; we are the sum of the Father's love for us and our real capacity to become the image of his Son." To become other Christs; to love as Christ loves; to see as Christ sees: this is our *real capacity*. But, as John Paul II tells us, when "the human heart is fixed in permanent suspicion, as is the case in Freudian hermeneutics"—or "if the Manichaean 'anti-value' is dominant in consciousness"—man is unable to tap into his "deepest and yet most real possibilities." He is unable to give voice to "the deepest layers of his potentiality . . . The ethos of redemption, by contrast, is based on a strict alliance with these layers" (TOB 49:6).

As John Paul II repeatedly insists, Christ's teaching "against the evil of concupiscence is at the same time an appeal to overcome it." Given this, "it follows that this victory must go hand in hand with an effort to discover the authentic value of the [body and sex], in order that the Manichaean 'anti-value' may not take root in man, in his conscience and will" (TOB 45:5). Precisely in this dimension of coming to "see" the true value of the human body and sex, Christ invites us to embark on a grand adventure: that of *reclaiming who we really are* as men and women made in the divine image. Precisely in this dimension of "seeing," Christ invites us to

> the rediscovery of the meaning of the whole of existence, of the meaning of life, which includes also the meaning of the body that we have called "spousal" here. The meaning of the body is in some way the antithesis of Freudian libido. The meaning of life is the antithesis of the hermeneutics 'of suspicion.' Such a *hermeneutics* is very different, *it is radically different* from the one we discover *in Christ's words* in the Sermon on the Mount. These words bring to light not only another ethos, but also another vision of man's possibilities. It is important that precisely in his "heart" [man] does not feel himself irrevocably accused and given up to the concupiscence of the flesh [as is the case in Freudian thought], but that in the same heart he feels himself called with energy. Called precisely to this supreme value, which is love. Called as a person in the truth of his humanity, and thus also in the truth of his masculinity and femininity, in the truth of his body. Called in that truth which has been his inheritance "from the beginning," the inheritance of his heart, which is deeper

> than the sinfulness inherited, deeper than the threefold concupiscence. Christ's words, set in the whole reality of creation and redemption, re-activate that deepest inheritance and give it real power in human life. (TOB 46:6)

Alleluia! Alleluia! Let us go make disciples of all nations! Let us go and become witnesses to our world—a world so terribly twisted in its view of the body, yet still yearning at the same time for all that is true, good, beautiful—let us witness to this world that *there is another way to see the body.* There is *another way to view and experience our sexuality.* Let us go and invite the whole world to "that fullness of 'eros,' which implies the upward impulse of the human spirit toward what is true, good, and beautiful, so that what is 'erotic' also becomes true, good, and beautiful" (TOB 48:1). But, oh!—if we ourselves do not even believe that such a transformation is possible, how can we become such witnesses?

We are not transformed overnight. As we all know well from experience, the journey is fraught with obstacles, temptations, painful falls and setbacks; but also, by God's mercy and grace, through it all, we can make significant progress and come to enter into unforeseen and previously unimagined freedoms. The task of living the full truth of our sexuality "*can* be carried out," John Paul insists, and "it is truly worthy of man" (TOB 48:4). Without this living hope, what, then, do we have to offer the world when it comes to this vital realm of human life? A list of rules to follow? Oh! If we ourselves are blind to "the glory of God in the human body" (TOB 57:3), then who are we in relation to the world when it comes to sexuality but the blind leading the blind? Is this where we want to remain? Should we not instead cry out from the depths of our hearts with the blind men in the Gospel: "Have mercy on us, Son of David! . . . Lord, let our eyes be opened" (Mt 20:30, 33)?

It Is the Liturgy that Opens Our Eyes

All of us must contend to one degree or another with this "blindness" that obscures the true meaning and dignity of the body in its masculinity and femininity. It's a blindness that goes back to original sin, to the moment the first Adam disobeyed God. Then, with shock and horror, man and woman "saw" their nakedness through the prism of concupiscence *for the first time,* and covered themselves in shame (see Gen 3:7-10). John Paul II calls this "the 'second' discovery of sex" and observes that it "differs radically from the first" (TOB 29:4). Burdened by this inheritance, we've been hiding ever since. But, as we just heard from John Paul II, the inheritance of our hearts is *deeper than the sinfulness we've inherited,* deeper than our lusts and distortions. Christ reactivates that deepest inheritance and gives us *real power* to live from it!

The New Adam has risen from the first Adam's death, and in and through that resurrection-power he calls us to a new way of "seeing." Again, this is a journey—a long one, a difficult one, a painful one. Along the way of this journey, our vision only gradually "opens up." As Cardinal Ratzinger observes:

> At first the disciples did not recognize [the resurrected Christ]. They have to be led toward a new kind of seeing, in which their eyes are gradually opened from within . . . Perhaps the most telling episode of all is that of the disciples on the road to Emmaus. Their hearts are transformed . . . and at the breaking of the bread they experience in reverse fashion what happened to Adam and Eve when they ate from the fruit of the tree of the knowledge of good and evil; their eyes are opened. Now they no longer see just the

> externals but the reality that is not apparent to their senses yet shines through their senses. (SL, pp. 120-121)

Is this "seeing" only a gift for those disciples two thousand years ago? Or is it also a gift for us today? And how do they experience the "reversing" of that original blindness? Precisely through the liturgy! "The sacraments infuse holiness into the terrain of man's humanity: they penetrate the soul and body, the femininity and masculinity of the personal subject, with the power of holiness. All of this is expressed in the language of the liturgy" (TOB 117b:2). The Church's liturgy, beginning with the "nuptial bath" of Baptism, initiates us into the "redemption of our bodies" and life "according to the Spirit." As much "as 'concupiscence' darkens the horizon of interior vision and deprives hearts of the lucid clarity of desires and aspirations, so 'life according to the Spirit' . . . allows man and woman to find again the true freedom of the gift together with the awareness of the spousal meaning of the body" (TOB 101:5). This is a specific grace of the Sacrament of Marriage, John Paul tells us, but it is by no means a grace limited to married people. For, in the Sermon on the Mount, Christ invites all of us "to a pure way of looking at others, capable of respecting the spousal meaning of the body" (VS 15).

The more we grow in this pure way of "seeing," the more spousal symbolism illuminates for us "the entire Christian life," beginning with Baptism. But if "an interior opening-up does not occur in man that enables him . . . to perceive the reflection of divine glory in creation, then God remains excluded from our field of vision" (SL, p. 122). In such case, we'll stop at the surface of the "sexual sphere," and spousal symbolism will appear inappropriate, base, even perverse. Let us be patient with ourselves (and with others) as we journey towards this "interior opening up," for we face a formidable foe who is literally hell-bent on keeping us from this vision. But let us make the journey! The victor is not the one who is hell-bent on blinding us. The victor is Christ who came to undo the work of the devil and give sight to the blind. Oh, Lord, may our eyes be opened.

Endnotes

Introduction

1. My sabbatical was a much needed time of growth and renewal. In my zeal to spread the TOB, I had overextended myself. I needed time away from the demands of my work to reflect and pray, to be purified and humbled. In his teaching on the stages of purification through which we all must pass, St. John of the Cross observes that a soul may spend many years in a stable place of service to the Lord before the need for deeper purification presents itself (see *The Dark Night*, bk II, chap I, no. I). One of the dangers of this extended place of stability, he tells us, is that of becoming "too secure" in the progress we've made. To rescue us from this trap, God allows us to undergo various external and internal trials that reveal to us new depths of our own poverty. My sabbatical allowed me to embrace my spiritual poverty more fully. The journey continues, of course, but I will always be grateful to the Lord for the gift of that time and to various brothers and sisters in Christ who were beautiful witnesses to me of God's patience and mercy.
2. So as not to distract from this broader purpose of the book, details of the "TOB debate" are provided (for those interested) in the endnotes, rather than in the main body of the work. Furthermore, while I occasionally reference their ideas, other authors involved in the debate remain anonymous. I do not hesitate to acknowledge where I believe these authors have been correct in their critiques of my work. In being forthright about various mistakes I've made as a teacher along the way, perhaps other teachers and evangelists can avoid them. At the same time, an honest look at the issues also reveals where these authors have been mistaken. Those familiar with the conversation may know

who these authors are, but I have no desire to identify them for those who do not. For "everyone enjoys a natural right to the honor of his name and reputation" (CCC 2479).

Chapter 1

3. The complete text of the TOB contains 135 addresses (addresses 95b and 117b in the latest English edition make it appear to be 133). Ten addresses on the Song of Songs and the marriage of Tobias and Sarah were condensed into 4 for the Wednesday audience format. Hence, only 129 addresses were actually delivered. See HS pp. 6-8 and 13-14 for further explanation.
4. Except for italics added to some verses of Scripture, all italics in the statements quoted in this book belong to their original authors.
5. Some believe that in order to "raise the language" we should, in most cases, simply drop the word "sex." If we're speaking of our being male or female, we can just as easily say "gender" (although this word, too, is becoming very "fuzzy" in the modern world). And if we're speaking about sexual intercourse, we can refer to the "marital embrace," the "conjugal act," "spousal union," etc. These are all fine terms. I use them often. However, these "elevated terms," while helpful for some, present obstacles for others. More than a few people have found themselves wondering what I meant when I used terms like "marital embrace" or "conjugal union." As one student said in frustration: "*If you meant sex, why didn't you just say so?*"
6. Qualifiers such as "in some way" are, of course, important. Man's experience of "being a body"—while intrinsically related to sexuality—is not plainly and simply synonymous with it. We "cannot define [bodiliness] simply in terms of sexuality," to quote Pope Benedict XVI, "but sexuality is an essential component of bodiliness" (LW, p. 103).
7. Karol Wojtyla writes that everyone "belongs from birth to one of the two sexes. This fact is not contradicted by [those rare

cases of] hermaphroditism—any more than any other sickness or deformity militates against the fact that there is such a thing as human nature" (LR, p. 47).

8. As we all know, when sexual matters are removed from their proper, sacred context, they degenerate very quickly. For example, theological truths regarding intimate matters such as original nakedness (Gen 2:25), the blessing of fertility (Gen 1:28), the "abundant breasts" of the New Jerusalem (Is 66:11), or the spousal symbolism of the Church's liturgical life (Eph 5:25-32) can easily appear profane when removed from their sacred context (*pro fanum* means to remove from or "place in front of" the temple, the sacred place).
9. Movies often explain their "R" rating with the expression: "Contains sexuality." This is a perfect example of how our culture has reduced the richness of this word to a distorted (read: lustful) version of "sexual activity." If we understand the word correctly, our response to the statement "Contains sexuality" might be—*What? Are there men and women in the movie?*

Chapter 2

10. Some authors seem reluctant to recognize the continued, widespread influence of puritanism on the way people today—both inside and outside the Church—approach the body and sexuality. They insist that it's the pornographic vision of the body that holds sway today, not the puritanical one. While there is a certain point to this idea, it also fails to recognize the close relationship of the two. As Professors Sarracino and Scott observe in their book *The Porning of America*, "Pornography . . . typically has an essentially Puritan point of view on sensuality and sex." We need only observe the "vocabulary of the typical Internet porn site . . . Sex is *sinful! Nasty! Naughty!* The only difference in this regard between the Puritans and the pornographers is that from the same starting point they go not merely in different, but in opposite, directions. Porn revels in what Puritanism rejects"

(pp. 5-6). The prevalence of pornography is not proof that the puritanical ethos is all but dead. Quite the contrary, it's proof that it's alive and well, albeit in morphed form.

11. Interview with Cathleen Falsani, somareview.com, 7/3/2006.
12. Ibid.
13. vanityfair.com/culture/features/2010/08.
14. dailybruin.com/news/2003/jan/15/sexual-aging/.
15. foxnews.com/story/0,2933,518219,00.html.
16. It seems to me that something similar may be in the air when people react indignantly to my compassion for Hugh Hefner. Granted, the way *Nightline* sensationalized my comments about Hefner in a 2009 interview caused confusion and, quite understandably, made many Catholics recoil. I had shared with the reporter that I was first educated about sex by Hugh Hefner, but was later rescued from that terribly destructive education by John Paul II. *Nightline* reported, instead, that John Paul II and Hugh Hefner were my "two big heroes." Mercy . . . I also shared with the reporter what I consider to be an intriguing historical connection between these two men: right at the same time Hefner started *Playboy* magazine—in the early 1950s—Karol Wojtyla started sharing the biblical vision that would eventually flower in his TOB. Is that merely a historical coincidence? Or can we see the Author of history at work? God did not leave us orphaned in our hour of need, but was already raising up a future pope to save us from the moral and cultural ruin to which pornography would lead. That's the "historical connection" I see, but the context was totally missing in what *Nightline* aired. I was naïve to think the secular media would correctly convey my comments, and for that I can only express my regret.
17. The key word here is "beginning." I can see how in some ways over the years, through my own pride, I became "too secure" in this healing. As a result, I came to believe I had some sort of "strength" to offer the Church and the world. The Lord, in his mercy, has been helping me see that all I *really* have to

offer is my weakness. To this end, I have found St. Thérèse of Lisieux's teaching of great benefit. Pope Pius XII summed up her insights well when he wrote: "We must take St. Thérèse at her word when she invites the most unregenerate as well as the most perfect to count nothing of value before God, save the radical weakness and spiritual poverty of a sinful creature" (Message of July 11, 1954). "The Lord is not discouraged by human weakness," John Paul II tells us. Rather, he responds "by proposing a more stable and intimate union" (address April 24, 1996). Speaking from experience, it seems only through various (painful) trials, in which our poverty becomes undeniable, do we come to accept that God's grace is sufficient for us, that his power is made perfect in our weakness (see 2 Cor 12:9), and that he is "rich in mercy" (Eph 2:4).

18. See TOBE, pp. 122-123, 189-192, 270-271, 287 for a further discussion of this healthy sense and positive role of shame.

19. Originally, all the figures were nude, but a pupil of Michelangelo, Daniele da Volterra, was commissioned to cover some of them with loincloths. This earned him the nickname "the maker of breeches." Over the next two centuries, various other veils and draperies were added. With the restoration project commissioned by John Paul II, Daniele da Volterra's additions were retained as part of the history of the painting, but all other loincloths were removed.

Chapter 3

20. *Super primam epistolam ad corinthios,* Lectura I, 10.

21. See William E. May, "Anthropology and Morality: Bodily Life as a Good Intrinsic to Persons and the Absolute Inviolability of Innocent Human Life," in *The Splendour of Life: Gospel, Science, and Ethics—Perspectives for Bioethics Ten Years After Evangelium Vitae (Lo Splendore della Vita: Vangelo, Scienza, ed Etica),* eds. Livio Melina and José Noriega (Vatican City: Pontifical Lateran University, 2006), pp. 457-476.

Chapter 4

22. One theologian writes that "we should expect holiness to 'trump' temptations or disordered tendencies in the area of sexuality exactly as often as we should expect holiness to 'trump' the reality of having to undergo death." If by "trump" this person means "eliminate," he makes a valid point. Holiness certainly does not *eliminate* temptations or our disordered tendencies in this life. But "trump" typically means to "overcome," "get the better of," "surmount," or "surpass." And if this person actually believes that the pull of concupiscence is just as insurmountable in this life as is death, then he is very far from the teaching of John Paul II. Or, at a minimum, he is using words very differently than John Paul II does.
23. "Although Christ did not come to give us coping mechanisms for sin, so long as we live in the historical tension of the 'already, but not yet' of redemption, we still need them. But if many spiritual advisors seem to focus on the 'not yet,' John Paul is at pains to balance this with the 'already'" (TOBE, p. 214).
24. When it comes to John Paul's teaching on "mature purity of heart," I can make the Little Flower's words my own: "I am very far from practicing what I understand" (SOS, p. 227). Of course, if we preach a gospel that only corresponds to our own practice, we will never preach the full demands of the Gospel—for no one in this life is without need of ongoing growth and purification. As the *Catechism* observes, "In everyone, the weeds of sin will still be mixed with the good wheat of the Gospel until the end of time" (CCC 827). These weeds have deep roots in us. I believe some authors have been correct in pointing out that I have not always emphasized this point enough.
25. Based on the ambiguity of the historical facts, I have come to agree with those who have pointed out that the story of Nonnus and Pelagia is not the best one to use in this context (some reports of their encounter make quite a different point than the

one I make). Still, the point that mature purity involves more than "looking away" remains valid regardless of what may or may not have happened between these two saints.

26. A faulty translation of John Paul II's catechesis has contributed to some confusion in this area. Michael Waldstein is currently working on a revision of his 2006 English translation based on the original Polish text rather than the Italian. As Waldstein shared with me in a private correspondence, the Italian word "*continenza*" was used to render a number of Polish words that should have been translated differently. For example, the expression "the virtue of continence" which appears several times in the current TOB translation, should have been rendered "the virtue of temperance." To speak of "the virtue of continence" is actually a contradiction in terms for a Thomist like John Paul II. This led me (incorrectly) to conclude that John Paul II used the word "continence" differently than did St. Thomas (see TOBE, pp. 565-566) when, in fact, John Paul II's actual expression, "the virtue of temperance," is entirely in keeping with St. Thomas. In article 4 of question 155, (II-II) of the *Summa,* Thomas observes that "temperance is much fuller than continence . . . because by temperance the sensory appetite itself is subordinated and as it were wholly possessed by the mind, whereas with continence its low desires remain rebellious. To sum up," says St. Thomas, "continence is to temperance as the unripe to the fully mature."

27. If we want to use the word "virtue" to mean "doing the commendable thing" or "doing the right thing," then the bishop who looked away also acted "virtuously." But in such a case we would be departing from the teaching of St. Thomas.

28. Some Catholics seem to want me to recommend self-flagellation and hair shirts in our battle with concupiscence. While these extreme forms of mortifications have their place in the tradition of the Church, our understanding of such practices must be balanced with advice such as this, which also has its place in the tradition of the Church: "The contemplative work of love by itself will

eventually heal you of all the roots of sin. Fast as much as you like, watch far into the night, rise long before dawn, discipline your body, and if it were permitted—which it is not—put out your eyes, tear out your tongue, plug up your ears and nose, and cut off your limbs; yes, chastise your body with every discipline and you would still gain nothing. The desire and tendency toward sin would remain in your heart" (*The Cloud of Unknowing*, 63).

29. Years of enduring trials and temptations, of falling and rising in my own life have certainly confirmed this teaching of the *Catechism* on the "long and exacting" work of growing in self-mastery.
30. Holding these two truths together—fallen *and* redeemed—is yet another case of learning how to rest in the "tension" of the Catholic "both-and." It invites a necessary "push-back" when anyone emphasizes one truth at the expense of the other. Theologians call this tension the "already—but not yet" of redemption. The *not yet* aspect means we must be cognizant of the many distortions of our fallen nature and the ease with which we can be lured into temptations. The *already* aspect means there is also a power at work within us which is able to do "far more than we ever think or imagine," as St. Paul said (see Eph 3:20). *Both* truths must be properly held together.

Chapter 5

31. Having lacked this gentleness and patience at times, I can understand why some have occasionally found the language and imagery I've used a bit jarring. If teaching can be compared to dancing with one's students, I confess I was not a very graceful dancer when I started out. In my zeal to convey certain points, I'd often step on my partner's toes or dip her too abruptly, so to speak. I've become a better dancer over the years, but to all those whose toes I've bruised or whose hearts I have jolted because of my "bad dancing," I humbly apologize.
32. Recall that we are always obligated to see sexual love in light of the fullness and depth proper to it as an integral, spousal

reality (see TOB 10:2). Spousal love is sexual love, integrally understood—that is, spousal love is the full expression of the love between the sexes. And sexual love, if it is true to itself, is by nature spousal love. If it seems safer to some to say "spousal" rather than "sexual," that's fine—so long as we don't "de-sexualize" spousality, as certain kinds of piety are prone to do. But to say "sexual" is fine too, so long as we don't "de-spousalize" sexuality as our culture is prone to do.

33. By demonstrating the organic connection between John Paul II's TOB and the mystical theology of St. John of the Cross, Michael Waldstein reveals more clearly how the various original insights of John Paul II represent an organic development of the Catholic theological tradition and not a departure from it. See his Introduction in TOB, pp. 24-34.
34. For example, when asked where John Paul's TOB fits within the four pillars of the *Catechism*—the Creed, the Sacraments, the Moral Life, and the Life of Prayer—many teachers and theologians are quick to place it within the Moral Life. Others place it within the Sacraments. Neither is inappropriate, of course. They're just too limiting. In his TOB, John Paul gives us a spousal frame through which to view our whole faith—the Creed, the Sacraments, the Moral Life, and the Life of Prayer. As Michael Waldstein put it, the TOB "can thus serve as a John-Pauline lens for reading the *Catechism*" (TOB, p. 15).
35. This is a dramatic claim. For a more detailed exploration of these ideas, see the entirety of TOB 96 and read TOBE pp. 417-420.
36. John Paul II offers a detailed analysis of the "*manifold contents*" (TOB 105:6) of the sacramental sign of marriage in TOB 103-107. In short, all of married life, the very couple themselves—beginning with the exchange of marital consent and throughout their lives—serves as the sacramental sign of marriage. In turn, conjugal intercourse is meant to be a sign that encompasses and sums up (con-summates) the reality of marriage as a whole. But one cannot reduce the whole reality of the "sign" of marriage to the act of conjugal intercourse (see TOBE, pp. 463-476).

37. Again, we have to define terms to know what we're even talking about here. What does it mean, in common parlance, to "sexualize" something? Because the word "sexual" itself, in some people's minds, indicates a tainted reality, to "sexualize" something, in this case, would also indicate a degradation or defilement. But the sexual realm is tainted only by the impurity that we ourselves bring to it. "To the pure all things are pure" (Titus 1:15). And purity, John Paul II tells us, "is the glory of the human body before God. It is the glory of God in the human body, through which masculinity and femininity are manifested" (TOB 57:3). In this context, we can understand Christ's words about purity of heart as follows: Blessed are the pure in heart, for they shall see the mystery of God in and through the "visible sign" of the human body in its masculinity and femininity. Thus, it is precisely in Christ's masculine body—in his sexuality—that we see (or should see) the glory of God revealed.
38. As one rather scandalized person put it, speaking of "supernatural insemination" and "coital imagery" in relation to the Blessed Mother is "grossly irreverent and smacks of blasphemy."
39. I don't hesitate to acknowledge that in my earliest work, I sometimes failed to communicate some important distinctions when applying the spousal analogy—a flaw in my presentation and word choice that led, in some cases, to a blurring, however unintentional, of the distinction between physical and mystical realities and of the infinite distinction between Creator and creature. For example, in teaching that spousal union foreshadows something of the joy that awaits us in heaven, some believed I was saying heaven was going to be some kind of eternal "sexual union" with God. Needless to say, this was a clear lesson in learning how to state my points more clearly. Pope Benedict XVI makes this particular point when he teaches that *eros,* to the degree that it is purified, provides "not just fleeting pleasure, but a certain foretaste of the pinnacle of our existence, of that beatitude for which our whole being yearns" (DC 4).

40. If mystics like Teresa of Avila speak of the "ineffable joy" they experienced in prayer as "nuptial union" with the Lord (see NMI 33), isn't this only a dim shadow of what Mary must have experienced when "the power of the Most High" came upon her? Of course, we must show great reverence when approaching such sublime mysteries. For, as I warned in *Heaven's Song* "if we presume to reach out and 'touch' this mystery without the proper reverence, we can expect the fate of Uzzah who was 'struck down' when he reached out to touch the ark of the Old Covenant without the proper respect (see 2 Sam 6). How much more reverence is required if we are to 'touch' ... the ark of the New Covenant ... ?" Then I ask: "Does this perhaps explain why Joseph was afraid to take Mary into his home (see Mt 1:20)?" (HS, p. 92). Just like Joseph, however, we must work through our fears. For we, too, are called to take Mary "into our home." While we must certainly keep the mystery of Mary reverently veiled, in the tension of the Catholic "both-and," we can also "have confidence to enter ... by the new and living way which he opened for us through the veil" (Heb 10:19-20). "But how difficult it is for us sinners to have the freedom, the ability, and the light to enter such an exalted and holy place," says St. Louis de Montfort. "Some," he says, "the great majority—will stop short at the threshold and go no further. Others—not many—will take but one step into its interior. Who will take a second step? Who will take a third? Finally who will remain in it permanently?" (*True Devotion* 119, 263). I wouldn't be surprised if those given the grace and courage to enter beyond the threshold found both King David and St. Joseph, "son of David," dancing with wild joy before the Ark. *Oh Mary, conceived without sin, pray for us that we would have the grace and freedom to enter your mystery with reverent joy and dancing!*

41. This is a quote from the modern mystic Adrienne von Speyr cited by Michele Schumacher in her illuminating article "A Speyrian Theology of the Body" (see VMTB, p. 256). Dr. Schumacher continues:

> This very firm conviction [about the absolute necessity of the body in grasping Christianity] caused Adrienne to mourn what she esteemed in the Church of her time "an artificial de-corporalization" opposed to the truth of imbuing the flesh with the Spirit's truth. As a case in point, Adrienne points out the significance of Christ's nakedness on the Cross. "The loincloth was the beginning of the Church's not-wanting-to-see." We should be conscious, she continues, that it is the Church—and not the Lord—who covered up his nakedness. The Church may do so with good reason, Adrienne admits, "but she has too often forgotten that the Lord's nakedness exists." (VMTB, pp. 256-257)

42. In my desire to safeguard diligently the truth of the enfleshment of our faith, I have offered a consistent "push-back" against prevalent ideas (and prevalent forms of "piety") that tend in any way to dis-incarnate our faith. Inasmuch as I may have pushed too hard at times against a "hyper-spiritual" focus, I can understand why some claim to see a "hyper-physical" focus in my work. Once again, it is a matter of finding the right "tension" between what appear to be competing truths.
43. See Homily XII from *Homilies on Colossians.*
44. For one example, see *The Complete Works of St. Teresa of Avila,* Volume I, pp. 192-193 (Burns and Oats, 2002).
45. Mention is made of "the 'miracle of lactation' when Our Lady is said to have fed [St. Bernard] with a stream of milk from her breast" in *Butler's Lives of the Saints* (see p. 201 of the Burns and Oats edition, 1998). Some believe this to be a charming but baseless legend, but its repeated depiction in liturgical art lends it credibility. Search "the lactation of St. Bernard" on Google images for several examples.
46. See *True Devotion* nn. 156, 216, 264.
47. See FS, p. 60.

48. Saint Symeon the New Theologian experienced this kind of projection from others and wrote of it as follows:

> If, in your body, you have put on the total Christ, you will understand without blushing all that I am saying; but if of the immaculate garment, I am speaking of Christ, you have only put on a small piece to your soul, . . . how would you not blush, clad with soiled garments? When I utter these formidable words about holy members [of the body], and, with an enlightened mind consider all their glory, . . . you consider your own flesh, all soiled . . . that is why you project your shame on Christ and on me. (15th of his 58 *Hymns of Divine Love*)

Chapter 6

49. Of course, we mean this in the sense of making of the body a false god. There is a sense in which Christians do "worship the body"—the body of our Lord sacramentally present in the Eucharist. We also speak properly of a "divinization of the body" (see TOB 67), which is God's gratuitous raising up of man—body and soul—to participate in his own divine nature (see 2 Pt 1:4). The *Catechism* teaches that "man was destined to be fully 'divinized' by God in glory. Seduced by the devil, he wanted to 'be like God,' but 'without God, before God, and not in accordance with God'" (CCC 398). And precisely in preferring himself to God, man idolizes his own humanity, including his body.

50. Some Catholic authors seem unfamiliar or, at any rate, uncomfortable with John Paul II's discussion of this holy kind of "fascination" with the body. John Paul II believes that St. Paul is inviting spouses specifically to recover a holy "fascination" with the body and sexuality when he calls them to submit to one another "out of reverence for Christ" (Eph 5:21). This "reverence," he says, "is nothing other than a *spiritually mature form* of that reciprocal *fascination*, that is to say, of the man for femininity

and of the woman for masculinity, which reveals itself for the first time in Genesis 2:23-25." He even says that the "spiritual maturity of this fascination is nothing but *the fruit born of the gift of fear,* one of the seven gifts of the Holy Spirit" (TOB 117b:4).

The lovers in the Song of Songs express the same holy kind of "fascination" and serve as a model for all lovers: "On seeing the woman created by God, man's first words express wonder and admiration, or even better, the sense of fascination (see Gen 2:23). *And a similar fascination—which is wonder and admiration—* runs in fuller form through the verses of the Song of Songs" (TOB 108:5). And lest we be tempted to dis-incarnate this holy "fascination," John Paul maintains that the "point of departure as well as the point of arrival for this fascination—reciprocal wonder and admiration—are in fact the bride's femininity and the bridegroom's masculinity, in the direct experience of their visibility. The words of love spoken by both of them are therefore concentrated on the 'body' "(TOB 108:6).

He goes on to clarify—and this is a critical point—that this fascination towards the other's body is not just "the body" in an objectified sense, but an integrated "*attraction toward the other person*" (TOB 108:6). When John Paul II invites us to this kind of "fascination" he's inviting us to the integration of body and soul that enables us to see the body as a transparent sign of the "great mystery" hidden in God from all eternity.

51. The "almost" in this statement is very important. We must qualify such statements this way, John Paul II tells us, because the "spousal meaning of the body has not become totally foreign to [the] heart: *it has not been totally suffocated in it by concupiscence, but only habitually threatened*" (TOB 32:3).

52. Iconoclasm was also heavily influenced by the rise of Islam which considered all sacred images idolatrous. In the West, the Church has also suffered its own iconoclasm in many places from a conscious or unconscious effort to appease Reformation sensibilities, right up into the twentieth century. Cardinal

Ratzinger observes that this "new iconoclasm, which has frequently been regarded as virtually mandated by the Second Vatican Council . . . eliminated a lot of *kitsch* and unworthy art, but ultimately it left behind a void, the wretchedness of which we are experiencing in a truly acute way" (SL, p. 130).

53. Recall the teaching of the *Catechism* that "man needs signs and symbols to communicate . . . with God" (CCC 1146).

54. If it isn't already clear, I want to state that when I make such heartfelt pleas—"Lord, open our eyes!"—I'm including myself in the prayer. I do not hold myself out as one who "already sees." Each believer is like the blind man who, touched once by the Lord, came to see more clearly, but needed to be touched again (and again, and again, and again).

55. Some warn that talking so insistently about the theology of our bodies places too much emphasis on the body in a culture in which everything is body-centered. I certainly do not claim that I've gotten the balance just right, but when I hear statements like this I find myself thinking—*Isn't Christianity, also, in its own way, body-centered*? Indeed, *the body* of Christ is the very center of our life and worship, the source and summit of our faith. The body-centeredness of the culture is simply a cheap substitute for the body-centeredness we're all created for and long for. A pornographic culture has fixated itself on the sign (the body in its sexuality and call to union) and failed to see that to which the sign points: the mystical reality of "nuptial union" with the divine consummated in the Eucharist.

56. Many years ago I heard a story on a tape series about the life of St. Teresa of Avila that has stayed with me. The speaker reported that once, late at night, some of Teresa's fellow Carmelites came to the kitchen to inquire about a ruckus. They were somewhat scandalized to find their Mother Superior delighting noisily in some left-over partridge. Teresa looked up from her feast and explained, "When I fast, I fast. But when I eat partridge, *I eat partridge*."

Chapter 7

57. Personally, I thoroughly enjoy the scholarly approach to theology. I've been immersed in serious theological study my entire adult life. However, with all due respect for the important work done by academics, I must say I can relate to the frustration St. Francis Xavier expresses in his letter to St. Ignatius.

58. In this context, I'm reminded of an e-mail exchange I once had with a secular musician whom I admired. I was pleasantly surprised to discover that he had acquired one of my books in which I had quoted lyrics from his music. I wrote to him hoping to establish "an itinerary of friendship in a dialogue of truth." I was disheartened, however, when he wrote back saying, "I'm reading your book, but I'm not getting it . . . I don't speak Catholic." Those four words have haunted me since: *I don't speak Catholic* . . . How do we reach such people? Like any missionary in a foreign land, we must learn to speak the native language. Whatever the dangers of being misunderstood (even denounced by some), we need to translate the Gospel "into the speech and thinking of our time" (LW, p. 63).

59. And, as John Paul II observes, it is precisely the "spousal dimension" of God's love that helps us see what sin really is. When God's people break his covenant, it's not only an infraction against a law and a divine Legislator. It's an act of "unfaithfulness and betrayal: a blow that directly pierces [God's] heart as Father, Bridegroom, and Lord" (TOB 104:3).

60. Some Christians seem almost to make a virtue out of rejecting the culture and keeping catechesis entirely free of its influence. One author writes: "Christianity is for all times, and all places: it is not 'historically conditioned.' Therefore it is not necessary for any Catholic to adapt to our pop culture, or allow the world to set the agenda." I agree that the world does not set the agenda. Christ sets the agenda. And Christ's "agenda" is to meet us *right*

where we are in this "present world" and this "present time" (*saeculum*). Other authors warn their readers that there simply *must* be something wrong with any Christian who "praises" the culture rather (presumably) than vilifying it. But I'd submit that we should be eager to praise the culture whenever it gets something right—like a father or mother, perhaps, who is eager to praise a child who struggles with math, usually gets things wrong, but every so often gets a problem right. "Way to go! Good job! Keep going!" It's a way of affirming the wheat among the weeds and encouraging the wheat to flourish.

61. See Paul VI's Address to Artists of May 7, 1964; John Paul II's *Letter to Artists* of April 4, 1999; and Benedict XVI's Address to Artists of November 21, 2009.
62. A powerful example of this can be seen in the popular YouTube video in which a man is utterly overwhelmed by the sight of a double rainbow (search "double rainbow" on YouTube). As this "dart" of beauty penetrates him more and more deeply, he unabashedly sighs, moans, and weeps. Some explain away his behavior by concluding he was on drugs. He has insisted in several interviews that he was not.
63. The very term "rock and roll"—coined by DJ Alan Freed in the early '50s—came, some say, from a slang term for sexual (mis)behavior.
64. I write and teach with references to "rock" music only because that's the kind of music I grew up listening to. My goal, as I often tell my audiences, is not to make everyone a fan of *that* music, but to give people permission to take comfort in the soundtrack of their own lives, so to speak, the particular music that speaks to *their* hearts. It might be classical music, it might be opera or jazz, it might be country or hip-hop, or it might be Gregorian chant or praise and worship music—whatever it is, we all seem to have a "soundtrack" that has accompanied our lives, a form of music that moves our hearts in a particular way. And God can and often does speak to our hearts through *that* music.

65. One can observe that there seems to be a different (and perfectly acceptable, from a Catholic point of view) sensibility between John Paul II and Benedict XVI when it comes to popular music. While over the years John Paul II was entertained by (or took part in events with) artists like Bob Dylan, B. B. King, Chaka Khan, Ricky Martin, Jewel, Lou Reed, Alanis Morissette, and the Eurythmics, such events seem quietly to have ceased since the election of his successor. It is well known that Cardinal Ratzinger was skeptical about the merits of having Bob Dylan perform at a Eucharistic Congress. Indeed, he has expressed his uneasiness with rock music on more than one occasion (e.g., see SL, p. 148). I don't disagree with his basic assessment of the problems with such music.

Appendix I

66. For the record, I have *never* discussed this matter in front of an audience. It has only come up in a public forum once that I can recall, and I referred the person who asked the question to my book rather than addressing it openly. I would not even have addressed it in my book if it were not a real question for some people in today's world.
67. As I wrote in my book *Good News about Sex and Marriage*, "An important point of clarification is needed . . . Since the female orgasm, however, isn't necessarily linked to the possibility of conception, so long as it takes place within the overall context of an act of intercourse, it need not, in any absolute sense, be during actual penetration" (GNSM, pp. 90-91).
68. What Liguori means by "sodomitic emotion" seems not altogether clear. He may mean that a husband cannot engage in such behavior without intending (and/or experiencing) ejaculation. If that were the case, it would seem the term "sodomitic intention" (Jone uses this term) would have been clearer. Furthermore, if Liguori simply means "sodomitic intention," then one could argue—as do Jone and Merkelbach—

that, so long as one excludes the intention to ejaculate, one can engage in this form of foreplay with a clear conscience. But I hope it is possible to read other factors into Liguori's term. The word "emotion" seems to include the realm of interior feeling and disposition. Why would a couple be attracted to such behavior? What is going on within them? Is what they are feeling and attracted to a true human good? On this level—even if such behavior cannot be condemned based on the teleology of ejaculation—one can find plenty of other reasons that demonstrate why such behavior should be condemned.

Appendix II

69. One might conclude from the context of this statement that John Paul is speaking only about the liturgical rite of marriage itself—the Nuptial Mass in which a marriage takes place. Recall, however, that marriage provides "*the foundation of the whole sacramental order*" (TOB 95b:7) and is in some way the prototype of all the sacraments (see TOB 98:2). This means that marriage also provides the model for understanding the "great mystery" that unfolds in the Church's liturgy. For the entire mystery of our redemption has "clothed itself" in the "figure and form" of the primordial sacrament of marriage (see TOB 97:2).

70. Some theological minds seem uncomfortable using spousal categories—which is to say "sexual" categories, if we understand the term "sexual" integrally, as we are obligated to do (see TOB 10:2)—to explain the whole of Christian life. They grant that spousal language can help us understand *part* of the picture, but do not want to frame Christianity as a whole in such terms. The *Catechism,* however, in keeping with the mystical tradition, does not limit the spousal reality of Christ's love to certain aspects of the Christian life. Rather, it observes that "the entire Christian life" bears this spousal imprint (see CCC 1617). To be sure, spousal categories are not the *only* way to frame the Christian mystery. Other imagery is also important in understanding

Christ and his relationship with the Church. Those who want to safeguard this truth are certainly on solid ground. But so, too, are those who use spousal/sexual categories as a lens through which to view "the entire Christian life." We can recall here John Paul II's statement that the spousal mystery of Ephesians 5 offers us a "summa" of the teaching about God and man fulfilled in Christ (see LF 19).

71. The *Catechism* also makes reference to this symbolism when it states that "baptismal grace . . . has begotten us in the womb of the Church" (CCC 2040).

72. Monsignor Bux is Professor of Sacramental Theology at the University of Bari in Italy. He is also a Consultor of the Congregation for the Doctrine of the Faith, the Congregation for the Causes of Saints, and the Office for Pontifical Celebrations.

73. zenit.org/article-28767?I=English.

74. For the record, I have *never* used the word "phallic" in reference to the paschal candle.

75. Here is an example from one author that seems to lean in this Freudian direction. The context of what follows is a discussion about mothers breast-feeding in public. Based on the strength of his statements, it seems he simply cannot imagine the possibility of seeing a woman breast-feeding through any other lens than concupiscence. He writes:

    > In America men generally consider exposure of a woman's bosom provocative, and I assert that men who are trying to live chastely find such exposure inappropriate, not because they think the female body is evil, or because they have a sexual hang up, but because they find too much exposed flesh in that area, regardless of the context, sexually arousing. Period. I have been a guy for my whole life . . . I know well enough how men think. Women can pooh-pooh this all they want, but there is really nothing more complicated, sub-conscious or deep and dark about it than plain old male libido.

I am not advocating that women in our culture indiscriminately expose their breasts while nursing. However, it appears to me that we can recognize various dangers John Paul II warns about in the above sentiments. First of all, it is curious that what this author labels "inappropriate" is the woman's behavior rather than his own lust. While he doesn't claim that the woman's body itself is evil, he does subtly shift the blame in her direction rather than placing it squarely where it belongs: on the lusts of his own heart. The "great danger" here, as John Paul II tells us, is that the real evil—the lust in the heart—can be normalized and even justified because it is not called out, it is not taken to task (see TOB 45:4). "This is just the way men are," we are told. Or, as this author puts it, it's not a "sexual hang up" that causes men to lust in this way; "there is really nothing more complicated, sub-conscious or deep and dark about it than plain old male libido."

Hold on a moment. The "plain old male libido" I know of *is* "dark" in as much as it's riddled with selfishness, with lust. If this is the "plain old male libido" we're talking about, it is indeed a "sexual hang up," for "in the beginning it was not so." Such "plain old male libido" is in need of deep transformation. Many men fail to see this. They think their lustful libido is "just the way it is." In turn, they normalize and even justify their lustful "libido" to the detriment of the object of that "libido" (in marriage, for example, they will think it's acceptable to gratify such lusts with their wives). As John Paul II observes, "the essential error of the Manichaean ethos consists precisely in this" (TOB 45:4).

ABOUT THE COVER

The Unity Cross

The Unity Cross was originally designed in Brazil in 1960 by Fr. Angel Vicente Cerró of the Schoenstatt Movement, a Marian Apostolic movement of the Catholic Church. It depicts the Virgin Mary—the "woman" at the foot of the cross—as an icon of the Church and humanity, receiving the blood of the crucified Christ in a chalice. It is the moment of the mystical, spousal union of the New Adam and the New Eve (see pp. 120 to 123 for a discussion of this mystery).

The asymmetrical yet balanced shape of the cross is unique to Cerró's design. It expresses the tender, organic movements of Divine Providence.

The Unity Cross was adopted by Blessed Mother Teresa of Calcutta as a symbol for her community, and a large Unity Cross is prominent in the chapel of the motherhouse of the Missionaries of Charity in Calcutta, India. In 1981, it was given to Pope John Paul II by the Schoenstatt family after he was shot in Saint Peter's Square. According to Cardinal Secretary of State Agostino Casaroli, it was a comfort and companion for the Holy Father during that "trying hour."